Chapter 1: Understanding Psychotic Breakdown

Definition and Overview of Psychotic Breakdown

Psychotic breakdowns are complex and often misunderstood mental health conditions that can significantly impact individuals and their loved ones. In this subchapter, we will provide an accessible and comprehensive overview of psychotic breakdowns, including their definition, causes, symptoms, and potential treatment options. Whether you are a member of the general public seeking knowledge, a patient seeking to understand your own experience, a parent concerned about your child's well-being, or a caregiver supporting someone through a psychotic breakdown, this information will be invaluable in navigating this challenging terrain.

A psychotic breakdown, also known as a psychotic episode or psychosis, refers to a severe mental state characterized by a loss of touch with reality. During a psychotic breakdown, individuals may experience hallucinations, delusions, disorganized thinking, and altered perceptions of the world around them. These symptoms can be distressing, confusing, and disruptive to daily functioning.

The causes of psychotic breakdowns are multifactorial and can include genetic predisposition, environmental stressors, substance abuse, and certain neurological conditions. It is essential to understand that individuals experiencing a psychotic breakdown are not responsible for their condition and that seeking professional help is crucial for proper diagnosis and treatment.

Recognizing the symptoms of a psychotic breakdown is essential for early intervention and treatment. Common signs include hearing voices or seeing things that others cannot, having irrational beliefs or suspicions, exhibiting erratic or disorganized behavior, and experiencing intense mood swings. It is important to note that symptoms may vary from person to person and can be influenced by cultural, social, and personal factors.

Recovery from a psychotic breakdown is possible through a comprehensive and individualized treatment approach. Early intervention, medication, psychotherapy, and support from family and friends play crucial roles in the recovery process. With the right treatment and support, individuals with psychotic breakdowns can manage their symptoms, regain control over their lives, and pursue their goals and aspirations.

In conclusion, understanding the definition and overview of psychotic breakdowns is essential for the general public, patients, parents, and caregivers. By recognizing the signs, causes, and available treatment options, individuals affected by psychotic breakdowns can better navigate their journey towards recovery. With empathy, education, and support, we can work together to reduce the stigma associated with psychotic breakdowns and foster a more inclusive and compassionate society.

Prevalence and Incidence Rates

Understanding the prevalence and incidence rates of psychotic breakdown is crucial in order to grasp the true impact of this condition on individuals and society as a whole. In this subchapter, we will explore the numbers behind psychotic breakdown, shedding light on the frequency of occurrence and the factors that contribute to its development.

Psychotic breakdown is a serious mental health condition that affects a significant portion of the population. According to recent studies, approximately 3 in 100 people will experience a psychotic episode at some point in their lives. These numbers may appear alarming, but it is important to remember that the term "psychotic breakdown" covers a broad spectrum of symptoms and severity levels.

The incidence rates of psychotic breakdown vary across different populations and age groups. Research suggests that young adults between the ages of 18 and 24 are at a higher risk of experiencing their first psychotic episode. This vulnerable age range coincides with important life transitions, such as moving away from home, starting college, or entering the workforce. These stressors, combined with genetic and environmental factors, can contribute to the development of psychosis.

It is worth noting that prevalence rates of psychotic breakdown differ across cultures and regions. Some studies suggest that urban areas have higher rates of psychosis compared to rural regions. This could be attributed to the increased stress, social isolation, and exposure to environmental toxins that are more prevalent in urban settings. Additionally, certain cultural beliefs and attitudes towards mental health may influence the reporting and diagnosis of psychotic breakdown in different communities.

Understanding the prevalence and incidence rates of psychotic breakdown is essential not only for individuals experiencing symptoms but also for their families, friends, and caregivers. Recognizing the scope of the condition can help reduce stigma and promote early intervention and appropriate treatment options. By raising awareness about the prevalence of psychotic breakdown, we can encourage a more supportive and understanding society for those affected.

In the following chapters of this book, we will delve deeper into the causes, symptoms, and recovery options for individuals experiencing a psychotic breakdown. By gaining a comprehensive understanding of this condition, we can empower ourselves, patients, parents, and carers to navigate the challenges and seek the help and support needed for a successful recovery journey.

Common Symptoms of Psychotic Breakdown

When it comes to understanding and navigating psychotic breakdowns, it is essential to recognize the common symptoms that may indicate the presence of this mental health condition. Psychotic breakdowns can be a distressing and overwhelming experience for individuals, as well as their loved ones. By being aware of these symptoms, we can better identify when someone may be going through a psychotic breakdown and seek appropriate treatment and support.

One of the primary symptoms of a psychotic breakdown is hallucinations. These are perceptions that occur without any external stimulus. People experiencing hallucinations may see, hear, smell, taste, or feel things that others cannot perceive. These hallucinations can be extremely vivid and real to the person going through them, often leading to confusion and fear. Recognizing hallucinations as a potential symptom of a psychotic breakdown is crucial to providing the necessary help and support.

Delusions are another common symptom of a psychotic breakdown. Delusions are false beliefs that individuals strongly hold despite evidence to the contrary. These beliefs can be bizarre and irrational, making it challenging for others to understand or reason with them. Delusions can cause individuals to become suspicious, paranoid, or even fearful of others around them. It is important to approach someone experiencing delusions with empathy and understanding, as their beliefs are genuinely real to them.

Disorganized thinking and speech are also typical symptoms of a psychotic breakdown. People may experience their thoughts racing or jumping from one unrelated topic to another. Their speech may become incoherent or jumbled, making it difficult for others to follow their train of thought. This disorganization can further contribute to feelings of confusion and frustration.

Changes in behavior and emotions are also indicators of a psychotic breakdown. Individuals may become increasingly withdrawn, agitated, or exhibit uncharacteristic behaviors. They may experience intense mood swings, ranging from extreme joy to profound sadness or anger. These changes in behavior and emotions can significantly impact daily functioning and relationships.

Recognizing these common symptoms of a psychotic breakdown is vital in order to seek appropriate treatment and support. If you or someone you know is experiencing these symptoms, it is crucial to reach out to a mental health professional who can provide a comprehensive evaluation and develop a tailored treatment plan. With the right support, understanding, and treatment options, individuals going through a psychotic breakdown can find hope, recovery, and improved quality of life.

Chapter 2: Causes of Psychotic Breakdown

Biological Factors

Understanding the complex nature of psychotic breakdowns requires us to explore the various factors that contribute to their development. One crucial aspect that cannot be overlooked is the role of biological factors. These factors encompass a range of genetic, neurochemical, and structural components that can significantly influence the onset and progression of psychotic symptoms.

Genetics play a fundamental role in the development of a psychotic breakdown. Research has shown that individuals with a family history of psychotic disorders are at a higher risk of experiencing a similar breakdown themselves. This suggests a genetic predisposition to these conditions, although it is important to note that genetics alone do not determine one's fate. Environmental factors, such as stress or substance abuse, can interact with genetic vulnerabilities to trigger a psychotic episode.

Another critical biological factor relates to neurochemical imbalances in the brain. Neurotransmitters, such as dopamine and serotonin, are responsible for transmitting messages between brain cells. When these neurotransmitters are disrupted, it can lead to disturbances in perception, thinking, and mood, all of which are characteristic of psychotic breakdowns. These imbalances can be caused by various factors, including genetic predisposition, drug use, or even hormonal changes during adolescence or pregnancy.

Structural abnormalities in the brain have also been associated with the development of psychotic symptoms. Brain imaging studies have revealed differences in the size and functioning of certain brain regions in individuals experiencing a psychotic breakdown. These differences are particularly evident in areas responsible for processing sensory information, emotions, and higher cognitive functions. While the exact relationship between brain structure and psychosis is still being explored, these findings suggest that certain structural variations may contribute to the vulnerability for experiencing a psychotic episode.

Understanding the biological factors involved in psychotic breakdowns is crucial for developing effective treatment options. Medications that target neurochemical imbalances, such as antipsychotics, can help alleviate symptoms and prevent future episodes. Additionally, early identification of genetic predispositions can allow for early intervention and prevention strategies to be implemented.

It is important to note that while biological factors play a significant role in the development of psychotic breakdowns, they are not the sole determinants. Environmental factors, such as trauma, social isolation, or substance abuse, can also contribute to the onset and severity of symptoms. A comprehensive understanding of all these factors is essential for providing holistic treatment and support to individuals experiencing a psychotic breakdown, as well as their families and caregivers.

Genetic Predisposition

Understanding the causes of a psychotic breakdown is crucial to providing effective treatment and support for individuals experiencing this challenging condition. One important factor that plays a significant role in the development of psychosis is genetic predisposition. In this subchapter, we will explore the influence of genetics on psychotic breakdown, shedding light on how our genes can contribute to the manifestation of symptoms, and what it means for patients, parents, and carers.

Genetic predisposition refers to an individual's susceptibility to developing certain conditions due to inherited genetic variations. Research has shown that there is a strong genetic component to the development of psychosis, meaning that individuals with a family history of the disorder are at a higher risk of experiencing a psychotic breakdown. Studies have indicated that having a first-degree relative, such as a parent or sibling, with psychosis significantly increases the likelihood of developing the condition.

Various genes have been identified as potential contributors to the development of psychosis. These genes are involved in processes such as neurotransmitter regulation, brain development, and immune system functioning. However, it is important to note that genetic predisposition alone does not determine whether an individual will develop psychosis. Environmental factors, such as stress, trauma, substance abuse, and social isolation, also play a significant role in triggering the onset of symptoms.

Understanding one's genetic predisposition to psychosis can be empowering for patients, parents, and carers. It allows for early detection and intervention, which can significantly improve outcomes and prevent further deterioration. Genetic testing, in combination with comprehensive clinical assessments, can provide valuable insights into an individual's risk profile and guide treatment decisions.

For parents and carers, having knowledge about genetic predisposition can help in recognizing early warning signs and seeking appropriate support. It is important to remember that genetic predisposition does not guarantee the development of psychosis, but it does highlight the need for proactive measures. Creating a supportive and nurturing environment, promoting healthy coping strategies, and fostering open communication are vital to managing the risk of a psychotic breakdown in individuals with a genetic predisposition.

In conclusion, genetic predisposition is a crucial aspect of understanding the causes of psychotic breakdown. While genetics alone do not determine the development of psychosis, they play a significant role in increasing an individual's vulnerability. By recognizing this predisposition and taking appropriate steps, such as genetic testing and early intervention, patients, parents, and carers can navigate the challenges of psychosis more effectively and improve the chances of successful recovery.

Neurochemical Imbalances

In the realm of mental health, neurochemical imbalances play a significant role in the development and progression of psychotic breakdowns. Understanding these imbalances is crucial for individuals and their loved ones seeking to navigate the complexities of this condition. This subchapter aims to shed light on the connection between neurochemical imbalances and psychotic breakdowns, providing valuable insights for the general public, patients, parents, and carers.

At its core, a psychotic breakdown refers to a period of severe mental distress characterized by hallucinations, delusions, disorganized thinking, and a loss of touch with reality. While the exact causes of psychotic breakdowns are still being explored, researchers have identified neurochemical imbalances as a key contributing factor.

Neurotransmitters, the chemical messengers in our brain, play a vital role in regulating our thoughts, emotions, and behaviors. In individuals experiencing a psychotic breakdown, there is often an imbalance in these neurotransmitters, particularly dopamine and glutamate. Dopamine, involved in reward-motivated behavior and the processing of emotions, is found to be excessively active during psychotic episodes. Conversely, glutamate, responsible for cognitive functions and information processing, is found to be deficient.

This neurochemical imbalance disrupts the delicate equilibrium necessary for healthy brain function, leading to the manifestation of psychotic symptoms. While the exact triggers for this imbalance are still being studied, factors such as genetic predisposition, environmental stressors, drug use, and trauma have been identified as potential contributors.

Understanding the role of neurochemical imbalances in psychotic breakdowns is crucial for effective treatment and recovery. Medications known as antipsychotics are commonly used to rebalance neurotransmitter levels and alleviate symptoms. These medications work by targeting dopamine receptors and reducing its activity, thus restoring equilibrium in the brain.

However, it is important to note that neurochemical imbalances are just one piece of the puzzle when it comes to understanding and treating psychotic breakdowns. Psychological therapies, such as cognitive-behavioral therapy (CBT) and psychoeducation, are also essential components of comprehensive treatment plans. These therapies aim to help individuals develop coping strategies, improve insight into their condition, and foster a sense of empowerment in managing their symptoms.

By understanding the role of neurochemical imbalances, individuals, parents, and carers can gain a deeper insight into the causes and progression of psychotic breakdowns. This knowledge empowers them to seek appropriate treatment options and support their loved ones effectively on the path to recovery.

Structural Brain Abnormalities

Understanding the underlying causes and mechanisms behind psychotic breakdowns is crucial for both patients and their support network. One significant area of research that has shed light on this topic is the study of structural brain abnormalities. These abnormalities refer to any physical changes or irregularities in the brain's structure that can contribute to the development and manifestation of psychotic symptoms.

Research has shown that individuals experiencing psychotic breakdowns often exhibit various structural brain abnormalities. These can include alterations in the size and shape of specific brain regions, changes in the connectivity between different brain areas, and abnormalities in the overall brain structure.

One common finding is the presence of enlarged ventricles in the brains of individuals with psychosis. Ventricles are fluid-filled spaces in the brain, and their enlargement has been linked to a loss of brain tissue. This loss may disrupt the normal functioning of neural circuits involved in cognitive processes, emotion regulation, and sensory perception, leading to the emergence of psychotic symptoms.

Additionally, studies have identified abnormalities in specific regions of the brain, such as the prefrontal cortex and hippocampus. The prefrontal cortex plays a crucial role in decision-making, social behavior, and cognitive functions, while the hippocampus is involved in memory formation and emotion regulation. Changes in these regions may contribute to the cognitive and emotional difficulties experienced by individuals during a psychotic breakdown.

It is important to note that structural brain abnormalities are not the sole cause of psychotic breakdowns. They are just one piece of the complex puzzle that includes genetic predispositions, environmental factors, and other biological markers. However, understanding these abnormalities can help researchers and clinicians develop targeted treatments and interventions to alleviate symptoms and promote recovery.

While this research is promising, it is essential to remember that each individual's experience is unique, and not everyone with structural brain abnormalities will develop psychosis. Furthermore, not all individuals experiencing a psychotic breakdown will show these specific brain abnormalities. Therefore, it is crucial not to make assumptions or stigmatize individuals based solely on brain structure.

In conclusion, exploring structural brain abnormalities provides valuable insights into the causes and mechanisms of psychotic breakdowns. Understanding these changes in the brain's structure can aid in the development of effective treatment options and support strategies for individuals experiencing psychosis. However, it is important to approach this information with caution and recognize the complexity and diversity of mental health experiences.

Environmental Factors

Environmental factors play a crucial role in the development and progression of psychotic breakdowns. While genetic predisposition and brain chemistry are important factors, it is essential to understand how the environment can influence the onset, severity, and recovery of these episodes. This chapter explores various environmental factors that can contribute to psychotic breakdowns and provides insights for individuals, parents, and caregivers seeking to support someone during their journey of recovery.

Stress is a significant environmental factor that can trigger or worsen psychotic symptoms. High levels of stress, whether from work, relationships, or traumatic experiences, can overload the brain's capacity to cope, leading to a breakdown. It is important to identify sources of stress and develop effective coping mechanisms to reduce its impact. Encouraging relaxation techniques such as meditation, deep breathing exercises, and engaging in hobbies can help manage stress levels.

Another environmental factor to consider is substance abuse. Substance use, including alcohol, marijuana, or other illicit drugs, can significantly increase the risk of experiencing a psychotic breakdown. These substances can alter brain chemistry, disrupt cognitive functioning, and exacerbate existing symptoms. It is vital for individuals, especially those with a history of psychosis, to avoid substance abuse and seek professional help if struggling with addiction.

The social environment also plays a crucial role in psychotic breakdowns. Isolation, loneliness, and poor social support can contribute to the development and worsening of symptoms.

Maintaining a strong support system, participating in social activities, and fostering healthy relationships can provide a protective factor against psychotic breakdowns. Additionally, educating friends, family, and colleagues about psychosis can help create a supportive and understanding environment.

Physical health and lifestyle choices also impact the occurrence and severity of psychotic breakdowns. Lack of sleep, poor nutrition, and sedentary lifestyle can negatively affect mental health and increase vulnerability to breakdowns. Prioritizing adequate sleep, a balanced diet, and regular exercise can improve overall well-being and potentially reduce the risk of psychotic episodes.

Finally, the physical surroundings can influence the course of psychosis. A chaotic, disorganized, or stressful living environment can contribute to feelings of instability and exacerbate symptoms. Creating a calm and structured home environment can provide a sense of security and stability, aiding in recovery.

Understanding these environmental factors is crucial for individuals experiencing psychotic breakdowns, as well as their families and caregivers. By addressing these factors and making appropriate changes, individuals can enhance their chances of recovery and reduce the likelihood of future episodes. With proper support, education, and a conducive environment, individuals can navigate through their psychotic breakdowns and work towards leading fulfilling and productive lives.

Traumatic Experiences

In the journey of navigating a psychotic breakdown, understanding the role of traumatic experiences is crucial. Trauma can have a profound impact on an individual's mental health, and recognizing its significance is essential for both patients and their support system. This subchapter aims to shed light on the relationship between traumatic experiences and psychotic breakdowns, offering insights into causes, symptoms, and possible recovery options.

Traumatic experiences encompass a wide range of events that can deeply affect an individual's sense of safety and well-being. These can include physical or emotional abuse, neglect, accidents, natural disasters, or witnessing violence. For some individuals, such events can act as triggers, leading to the development of a psychotic breakdown. It is important to note that not everyone who experiences trauma will develop psychosis, but it is a risk factor that cannot be ignored.

The connection between trauma and psychosis lies in the impact on the brain and the subsequent development of coping mechanisms. Trauma can disrupt the brain's normal functioning and lead to changes in the way it processes information. This can result in the emergence of symptoms such as hallucinations, delusions, and disorganized thinking. Moreover, traumatic experiences can also exacerbate existing mental health conditions, making recovery more challenging.

Recognizing the symptoms of trauma-related psychosis is crucial for early intervention and treatment. These symptoms may include flashbacks, nightmares, hypervigilance, emotional numbness, and avoidance of triggers. By understanding the connection between trauma and psychosis, individuals can seek appropriate support and resources to address their specific needs.

Recovery from trauma-related psychotic breakdowns is a complex and multifaceted process. It requires a holistic approach that integrates therapy, medication, and a supportive environment. Therapeutic interventions, such as cognitive-behavioral therapy (CBT) and trauma-focused therapy, can help individuals process their traumatic experiences and develop healthier coping mechanisms. Medication, under the guidance of a psychiatrist, may also be necessary to manage symptoms and stabilize mood.

For patients, parents, and carers, it is essential to create a safe and nurturing environment that promotes healing and recovery. This can involve providing emotional support, encouraging open communication, and actively participating in the treatment process. Additionally, educating oneself about trauma and psychosis can empower individuals to advocate for their own well-being or that of their loved ones.

In conclusion, traumatic experiences can significantly impact an individual's mental health and increase the risk of developing a psychotic breakdown. By understanding the connection between trauma and psychosis, individuals can seek appropriate support and resources to address their needs. Recovery from trauma-related psychotic breakdowns requires a comprehensive approach that integrates therapy, medication, and a supportive environment. With awareness, knowledge, and a compassionate support system, individuals can navigate their way towards healing and regain control over their lives.

Substance Abuse

Substance abuse is a significant factor that can contribute to the development and worsening of psychotic breakdowns. In this subchapter, we will explore the relationship between substance abuse and psychotic breakdowns, the impact it has on individuals, and the available treatment options.

To begin, it is crucial to understand what substance abuse entails. Substance abuse refers to the misuse and excessive consumption of substances such as alcohol, illicit drugs, prescription medications, or even legal substances like nicotine or caffeine. These substances can alter brain chemistry, leading to various mental health issues, including psychotic breakdowns.

The association between substance abuse and psychotic breakdowns is well-documented. Research has shown that individuals who abuse substances are at a higher risk of experiencing psychotic symptoms compared to those who do not engage in substance misuse. The use of certain drugs, such as cannabis or hallucinogens, can trigger or exacerbate psychotic symptoms, leading to a full-blown psychotic breakdown.

Substance abuse can also worsen the course and outcome of a psychotic breakdown. It can lead to a more severe illness, increased hospitalizations, and reduced response to treatment. Moreover, substance abuse can hinder the effectiveness of medications prescribed to manage psychotic symptoms, making it more challenging for individuals to recover.

For patients, parents, and carers, it is crucial to be aware of the signs and symptoms of substance abuse. Some common indicators include changes in behavior, drastic mood swings, social withdrawal, decline in school or work performance, and neglecting personal responsibilities. If you suspect substance abuse in yourself or someone you care for, it is important to seek professional help promptly.

Treatment options for individuals struggling with substance abuse and a concurrent psychotic breakdown are available. Integrated treatment approaches that address both the substance abuse and the underlying mental health condition are most effective. These treatments may include medication management, individual and group therapy, family therapy, and support groups.

In conclusion, substance abuse is a significant contributor to the development and worsening of psychotic breakdowns. Understanding the relationship between substance abuse and psychotic symptoms is crucial for the general public, patients, parents, and carers. By recognizing the signs of substance abuse and seeking appropriate treatment, individuals can significantly improve their chances of recovery and manage their mental health effectively.

Stress and Trauma

Stress and Trauma: Understanding their Role in Psychotic Breakdown

In the journey of understanding and navigating psychotic breakdowns, it is crucial to delve into the factors that contribute to their occurrence. One such critical aspect is the relationship between stress, trauma, and the onset of psychotic symptoms. This subchapter aims to shed light on the impact of stress and trauma on individuals experiencing a psychotic breakdown, providing valuable insights for the general public, patients, parents, and caregivers.

Stress, an inevitable part of life, encompasses various challenges that can strain our mental and emotional well-being. However, excessive or prolonged stress can overwhelm an individual's coping mechanisms, potentially leading to a breakdown in their psychological functioning. In the context of psychotic breakdown, stress has been identified as a triggering factor, amplifying existing vulnerabilities and increasing the risk of developing symptoms such as delusions, hallucinations, and disorganized thinking.

Moreover, trauma can significantly contribute to the development of a psychotic breakdown. Traumatic experiences, such as physical or sexual abuse, neglect, or witnessing a distressing event, can deeply impact an individual's mental health. Trauma often creates a fertile ground for the emergence of psychotic symptoms, as it disrupts the person's sense of safety, trust, and stability. Understanding the role of trauma in psychotic breakdowns is crucial, as it emphasizes the need for trauma-informed approaches to treatment and support.

For individuals experiencing a psychotic breakdown, stress and trauma can exacerbate symptoms and hinder recovery. Recognizing the importance of stress management techniques and trauma-focused interventions is vital for patients, parents, and caregivers. Learning effective coping strategies, such as mindfulness, relaxation exercises, and seeking support from mental health professionals, can help individuals navigate the challenges associated with stress and trauma, potentially reducing the severity and frequency of psychotic symptoms.

Additionally, this subchapter aims to promote awareness among the general public, dispelling misconceptions and reducing stigma surrounding psychotic breakdowns. By understanding the complex interplay between stress, trauma, and psychotic symptoms, society can foster a more compassionate and inclusive environment for those experiencing mental health challenges.

In conclusion, stress and trauma play significant roles in the occurrence and exacerbation of psychotic breakdowns. Acknowledging their impact and implementing appropriate interventions is crucial for individuals navigating this complex journey. By addressing stress, trauma, and their implications, this subchapter aims to empower patients, parents, caregivers, and the general public in their quest for understanding, supporting, and recovering from psychotic breakdowns.

Chapter 3: Recognizing Symptoms of Psychotic Breakdown

Positive Symptoms

Positive symptoms refer to the experiences and behaviors that are not present in individuals without a psychotic disorder but are added to their mental state during a psychotic breakdown. These symptoms often make it challenging for individuals experiencing them to differentiate between reality and their distorted perceptions. In this subchapter, we will explore the various positive symptoms commonly associated with a psychotic breakdown, their potential causes, and the available treatment options.

One of the most recognizable positive symptoms is hallucinations. Hallucinations can occur in any of the five senses, with auditory hallucinations being the most common. People experiencing auditory hallucinations may hear voices speaking to them, often commenting on their thoughts or actions. Visual hallucinations, on the other hand, involve seeing things that are not there, while olfactory hallucinations involve smelling odors that have no basis in reality.

Another positive symptom is delusions, which are fixed false beliefs that are not influenced by rational arguments or evidence to the contrary. Delusions can be paranoid, such as believing that someone is out to harm them, or grandiose, where individuals have an exaggerated sense of their own importance or abilities.

Disorganized thinking and speech are also prevalent positive symptoms. People experiencing disorganized thinking may struggle with logical and coherent thoughts, making it difficult for others to understand their speech. Their speech may be disorganized, jumping from one topic to another without apparent connection.

Psychomotor disturbances are another positive symptom that may manifest as either agitation or catatonia. Agitation involves restlessness, pacing, and an overall inability to sit still. Catatonia, on the other hand, is a state of immobility and unresponsiveness.

The causes of these positive symptoms are not yet fully understood, but researchers believe that a combination of genetic, environmental, and neurobiological factors may contribute to their development. It is important to note that positive symptoms are not the result of personal weakness or character flaws.

Fortunately, there are various treatment options available for individuals experiencing positive symptoms. Antipsychotic medications can help reduce the intensity and frequency of hallucinations, delusions, and disorganized thinking. Psychotherapy, such as cognitive-behavioral therapy, can also be beneficial in helping individuals cope with and manage their symptoms.

In conclusion, positive symptoms are an integral part of a psychotic breakdown, often making it challenging for individuals to distinguish between reality and their distorted perceptions. Understanding these symptoms, their potential causes, and the available treatment options is crucial for individuals, their families, and caregivers. By providing support and appropriate treatment, individuals experiencing positive symptoms can work towards recovery and regain control over their lives.

Delusions

Delusions: Understanding the Intricacies of Psychotic Breakdown

Delusions are a common symptom of psychotic breakdowns, often associated with conditions such as schizophrenia, bipolar disorder, or severe depression. They are characterized by fixed false beliefs that are held with unwavering conviction, despite evidence to the contrary. Delusions can be distressing for individuals experiencing them and challenging for their families and caregivers to comprehend. In this subchapter, we aim to shed light on the nature of delusions, their causes, and available treatment options.

One of the most crucial aspects of understanding delusions is recognizing their various forms. Delusions can manifest in different ways, including paranoid delusions, grandiose delusions, somatic delusions, and religious delusions. Paranoid delusions involve irrational beliefs of persecution or being spied on, while grandiose delusions entail an exaggerated sense of self-importance or abilities. Somatic delusions revolve around false beliefs about the body, and religious delusions involve distorted perceptions of divine intervention or religious figures. By familiarizing ourselves with these forms, we can better grasp the complexity of delusions and their impact on individuals' lives.

The causes of delusions are multifaceted. They can arise from a combination of genetic predisposition, environmental factors, and abnormalities in brain chemistry. Stressful life events, trauma, substance abuse, or certain medications may also contribute to the development of delusions. Understanding these underlying causes can aid in early identification and intervention, potentially preventing a full-blown psychotic breakdown.

Fortunately, there are treatment options available for individuals experiencing delusions. The first line of treatment typically involves a combination of medication and psychotherapy. Medications such as antipsychotics can help alleviate the intensity and frequency of delusions, allowing individuals to regain control over their thoughts and perceptions. Psychotherapy, particularly cognitive-behavioral therapy (CBT), can assist patients in challenging and modifying their delusional beliefs, enabling them to develop more accurate and realistic perspectives.

Support from family, friends, and healthcare professionals is crucial for individuals navigating delusions. As a patient, parent, or caregiver, it is essential to educate oneself about delusions, their causes, and available treatment options. Patience, understanding, and empathy are vital when supporting someone experiencing delusions, as it can be a challenging and confusing experience for them.

In conclusion, delusions are a significant symptom of psychotic breakdowns, impacting individuals' lives and those around them. By understanding the various forms of delusions, their causes, and available treatment options, we can better support individuals experiencing these symptoms. Through education, empathy, and professional help, we can assist in the recovery process and provide a supportive environment conducive to healing and regaining a sense of normalcy.

Hallucinations

Hallucinations are one of the most distressing and misunderstood symptoms of a psychotic breakdown. They can be terrifying, confusing, and disorienting for both the individual experiencing them and those around them. In this subchapter, we will explore the nature of hallucinations, their causes, and the available treatment options.

Hallucinations are perceptual experiences that occur in the absence of any external stimulus. They can affect any of the senses, including hearing, seeing, smelling, tasting, and even feeling things on the skin. For example, a person may hear voices that others cannot hear or see objects or people that are not really there. These experiences can be so vivid and real that the individual may have difficulty distinguishing them from actual reality.

The causes of hallucinations during a psychotic breakdown are complex and multifaceted. They can be attributed to a combination of genetic, neurobiological, and environmental factors. Imbalances in certain neurotransmitters, such as dopamine, have been found to play a significant role in the development of hallucinations. Additionally, traumatic experiences, substance abuse, and extreme stress can also trigger hallucinatory episodes.

It is important to understand that hallucinations are not a sign of weakness or a character flaw. They are a symptom of an underlying condition and should be treated with compassion and understanding. If you or someone you know is experiencing hallucinations, seeking professional help is crucial.

Fortunately, there are various treatment options available to manage hallucinations and promote recovery. Medications, such as antipsychotics, can help reduce the intensity and frequency of hallucinations. Psychotherapy, including cognitive-behavioral therapy (CBT) and supportive therapy, can also be beneficial in helping individuals cope with and understand their hallucinations.

In addition to medical interventions, support from loved ones and a strong support network can make a significant difference in a person's recovery journey. Educating oneself about hallucinations and engaging in self-care practices, such as maintaining a healthy lifestyle, getting enough sleep, and managing stress, can also contribute to managing hallucinations effectively.

Remember, hallucinations are a treatable symptom, and with the right support and treatment, individuals can regain control over their lives and experience a fulfilling recovery. It is essential to approach hallucinations with empathy, provide a safe space for open communication, and seek professional help to ensure the best possible outcomes for those going through a psychotic breakdown.

Negative Symptoms

When it comes to understanding and navigating a psychotic breakdown, it is essential to familiarize oneself with the various symptoms that may arise. While many people are familiar with the positive symptoms of psychosis, such as hallucinations and delusions, there is another category of symptoms known as negative symptoms that are equally important to recognize and address.

Negative symptoms refer to a reduction or absence of normal emotional and behavioral responses that are typically seen in individuals without a psychotic disorder. These symptoms can have a significant impact on a person's ability to function and enjoy daily life. It is crucial for patients, parents, carers, and the general public to be aware of these symptoms in order to provide the necessary support and seek appropriate treatment options.

One common negative symptom is diminished emotional expression, which can involve a reduction in facial expressions, limited eye contact, and a lack of enthusiasm or interest in activities that were once enjoyed. This can make it difficult for individuals to connect with others and may lead to a sense of isolation or withdrawal from social interactions.

Another negative symptom is avolition, which refers to a lack of motivation or an inability to initiate and persist in goal-directed activities. Individuals experiencing avolition may struggle with basic daily tasks such as personal hygiene, household chores, or attending work or school. This can be distressing for both the individual and their loved ones, as it may lead to a decline in overall functioning and a loss of independence.

Alogia is another negative symptom characterized by a reduction in speech output or the quality of speech. People experiencing alogia may respond to questions with brief or vague answers, have difficulty initiating conversations, or exhibit a decreased flow of ideas. This can make communication challenging and may hinder the individual's ability to express themselves effectively.

It is important to note that negative symptoms are not always present in every individual experiencing a psychotic breakdown, and their severity can vary from person to person. However, recognizing and addressing these symptoms is crucial for the overall well-being and recovery of individuals affected by psychosis.

Treatment options for negative symptoms typically involve a combination of medication, psychotherapy, and support services. It is recommended that individuals seek professional help from mental health specialists who can provide a tailored treatment plan based on their specific needs and circumstances.

By understanding and acknowledging negative symptoms, patients, parents, carers, and the general public can play a pivotal role in supporting individuals experiencing a psychotic breakdown. By fostering empathy, education, and access to appropriate resources, we can help create a more compassionate and supportive environment for those navigating the complexities of psychosis.

Flat Affect

In the world of mental health, one term that often arises when discussing psychotic breakdowns is "flat affect." Flat affect refers to a state in which an individual displays limited emotional expression or appears emotionally unresponsive. It is commonly associated with various psychiatric disorders, including schizophrenia, major depressive disorder, and certain personality disorders.

Imagine encountering someone who seems devoid of emotional reactions, someone who rarely smiles or frowns, and whose facial expressions seem unchanging regardless of the situation. This person may have a flat affect. While it may be disconcerting to witness, it is crucial to understand that flat affect is a symptom of an underlying mental health condition, rather than a personal choice or indication of a lack of empathy.

The causes of flat affect are multifaceted and can vary depending on the individual and their specific condition. In schizophrenia, for example, flat affect is believed to stem from abnormalities in the brain's dopamine system, which plays a crucial role in regulating emotions. In cases of severe depression, a person may experience a reduction in their emotional responses due to the overwhelming weight of their symptoms.

Recognizing flat affect is essential, as it can help individuals and their loved ones seek appropriate support and treatment. Family members and caregivers may notice that the person appears detached or disinterested, struggling to express themselves emotionally, or finding it challenging to engage in social interactions. It is crucial to approach the situation with empathy and understanding, as these individuals may already be dealing with significant distress and confusion.

Treatment options for flat affect depend on the underlying condition causing it. In many cases, addressing the primary mental health disorder through therapy, medication, or a combination of both can help alleviate symptoms, including flat affect. Psychotherapy, such as cognitive-behavioral therapy (CBT), can assist individuals in recognizing and managing their emotions, while medication can help regulate brain chemistry and improve emotional responsiveness.

It is important to remember that recovery from flat affect, like any mental health symptom, is not a linear process. Each individual's journey is unique, and it may take time to find the right combination of treatments that work for them. Patience, support, and open communication are key when assisting someone experiencing flat affect.

In conclusion, flat affect is a symptom commonly associated with psychotic breakdowns and various mental health disorders. It is crucial to understand that it is not a personal choice or indication of a lack of empathy but rather a manifestation of an underlying condition. Recognizing flat affect and seeking appropriate treatment can help individuals regain their emotional responsiveness and improve their overall well-being.

Social Withdrawal

In the journey of navigating a psychotic breakdown, one common symptom that individuals may experience is social withdrawal. Social withdrawal refers to the tendency to isolate oneself from social interactions and activities. It can manifest as a gradual decline in social participation or a sudden withdrawal from social relationships altogether. This subchapter aims to shed light on the causes, symptoms, and possible treatment options for social withdrawal during a psychotic breakdown.

Causes of Social Withdrawal:
Social withdrawal can stem from various factors during a psychotic breakdown. Firstly, individuals may withdraw due to the distressing symptoms they experience, such as hallucinations or delusions. These symptoms can be overwhelming and make it difficult for individuals to engage in social interactions. Secondly, the stigma associated with mental health issues can lead to self-imposed isolation. Fear of judgment, misunderstanding, or societal discrimination often drives individuals to retreat from social situations. Additionally, the cognitive impairments that accompany a psychotic breakdown can make it challenging to engage in conversations or maintain relationships, further contributing to social withdrawal.

Symptoms of Social Withdrawal:
Recognizing the signs of social withdrawal is crucial to understanding its impact on individuals experiencing a psychotic breakdown. Some common symptoms include a loss of interest in previously enjoyed activities, declining invitations to social gatherings, and spending excessive amounts of time alone. Individuals may also exhibit changes in their communication patterns, becoming more reserved or avoiding conversations altogether. It is essential to note that social withdrawal can exacerbate feelings of loneliness, depression, and anxiety, potentially hindering the recovery process.

Treatment Options for Social Withdrawal:
Addressing social withdrawal requires a comprehensive approach that combines psychological, social, and medical interventions. Therapy, such as cognitive-behavioral therapy (CBT), can help individuals challenge negative thoughts and develop coping strategies to manage social anxiety. Social skills training can also be beneficial, providing individuals with the tools to navigate social situations more effectively. Additionally, involving support networks, such as family, friends, and support groups, can provide a sense of belonging and reduce feelings of isolation. Medications prescribed by a psychiatrist or healthcare professional may also be utilized to manage symptoms that contribute to social withdrawal.

In conclusion, social withdrawal is a common symptom experienced during a psychotic breakdown. Understanding its causes, recognizing its symptoms, and exploring treatment options are crucial steps towards supporting individuals on their journey to recovery. By fostering a compassionate and inclusive society, we can reduce the stigma surrounding mental health and provide the necessary support to those navigating a psychotic breakdown.

Cognitive Symptoms

When someone experiences a psychotic breakdown, it not only affects their perception and emotions but can also have a profound impact on their cognitive abilities. Cognitive symptoms refer to the changes in thinking, memory, concentration, and problem-solving abilities that can occur during a psychotic episode. In this subchapter, we will explore the cognitive symptoms commonly associated with a psychotic breakdown, their causes, and potential treatment options.

One of the most prominent cognitive symptoms experienced during a psychotic episode is difficulty with concentration and attention. Individuals may find it challenging to focus on tasks, keep their mind from wandering, or pay attention during conversations. This can lead to problems at work or school and can make it difficult to complete even simple daily activities.

Another cognitive symptom that often accompanies a psychotic breakdown is impaired memory. Individuals may struggle to recall recent events or conversations, have difficulty remembering tasks or appointments, or experience confusion about their past. This can be particularly distressing for both the individual experiencing the symptoms and their loved ones.

In addition to problems with concentration and memory, individuals may also experience difficulties with problem-solving and decision-making. They may struggle to organize their thoughts, find it hard to make logical connections, or feel overwhelmed when faced with complex situations. This can have a significant impact on their ability to navigate daily life and can contribute to feelings of frustration and helplessness.

The cognitive symptoms experienced during a psychotic breakdown can be caused by a variety of factors. Neurochemical imbalances in the brain, genetic predisposition, and environmental stressors can all contribute to these symptoms. It is crucial to remember that every individual's experience is unique, and the specific combination of factors affecting their cognitive abilities may differ.

Fortunately, there are treatment options available to address cognitive symptoms during a psychotic breakdown. Medications can help stabilize brain chemistry and alleviate some of the cognitive difficulties. Additionally, therapy and counseling can provide individuals with coping strategies to manage cognitive symptoms and improve overall cognitive functioning.

In conclusion, cognitive symptoms are a common aspect of a psychotic breakdown and can significantly impact an individual's daily life. Difficulties with concentration, memory, and problem-solving can be distressing and frustrating. However, with the right treatment and support, individuals can learn to manage these symptoms and regain control over their cognitive abilities. It is essential for patients, parents, and carers to understand these symptoms and explore the available treatment options to help facilitate recovery and improve overall quality of life.

Disorganized Thinking

Disorganized Thinking: Unraveling the Mysteries of Psychotic Breakdown

In the journey of understanding and navigating psychotic breakdowns, one of the most perplexing aspects is disorganized thinking. Imagine your thoughts as a well-organized library, where each idea has a designated shelf and logical connection. Now, picture that library in chaos, with books scattered haphazardly and ideas floating aimlessly. This is what individuals experiencing disorganized thinking go through, and it's essential to shed light on this topic to aid the general public, patients, parents, and carers in comprehending this intricate facet of psychotic breakdowns.

Disorganized thinking, or formal thought disorder, manifests as an inability to maintain a logical and coherent flow of thought. It often presents itself through disorganized speech, where sentences lack structure or fail to convey a clear message. Conversations may become challenging to follow, as individuals jump from one topic to another seemingly unrelated one. The connections between ideas might be tenuous or altogether absent.

This symptom can be profoundly distressing for those experiencing it, as well as their loved ones. It can hinder effective communication, making it difficult to express thoughts and feelings accurately. Moreover, disorganized thinking can contribute to social withdrawal, as the person may feel embarrassed or misunderstood.

The causes of disorganized thinking in psychotic breakdowns are multifaceted. They range from underlying genetic predispositions to environmental factors, such as stress or substance abuse. Disorganized thinking often emerges alongside other symptoms of psychosis, such as hallucinations and delusions. Understanding this interplay can help one grasp the broader context of psychotic breakdowns and how disorganized thinking fits into the puzzle.

While disorganized thinking poses unique challenges, recovery is possible with appropriate treatment and support. Psychotherapy, such as cognitive-behavioral therapy (CBT), can assist individuals in regaining control over their thoughts and improving communication skills. Medications, when prescribed by a qualified professional, can also alleviate symptoms and restore cognitive clarity.

For patients, parents, and carers, it is crucial to approach disorganized thinking with empathy, patience, and understanding. Educating oneself about this symptom can foster compassion and open up channels of constructive communication. By creating an environment that promotes acceptance and support, individuals experiencing disorganized thinking can feel empowered on their journey toward recovery.

In conclusion, disorganized thinking is a significant aspect of psychotic breakdowns that merits attention and understanding. By exploring this topic, we aim to equip the general public, patients, parents, and carers with the knowledge needed to navigate the complexities of disorganized thinking. Together, we can foster a society that embraces and supports individuals experiencing psychotic breakdowns, enabling them to reclaim their lives and thrive on their path to recovery.

Poor Concentration and Memory

One of the most common challenges individuals face during a psychotic breakdown is poor concentration and memory. This subchapter aims to shed light on this issue and provide useful information for the general public, patients, parents, and carers.

During a psychotic breakdown, individuals often experience a range of cognitive difficulties that can significantly impact their daily lives. Poor concentration and memory are two of the most prominent symptoms in this regard. Concentration refers to the ability to focus and sustain attention on a particular task or thought, while memory involves the ability to retain and recall information.

The causes of poor concentration and memory during a psychotic breakdown are multifaceted. The altered brain chemistry and disrupted neural pathways experienced during psychosis can directly impact cognitive functioning. Additionally, the distressing symptoms associated with psychosis, such as hallucinations and delusions, can be highly distracting and make it difficult to concentrate or remember things.

It is crucial for individuals experiencing poor concentration and memory during a psychotic breakdown to seek appropriate treatment and support. Medications, such as antipsychotics, can help stabilize brain chemistry and improve cognitive functioning. Additionally, therapy and rehabilitation programs aimed at enhancing cognitive skills can be highly beneficial.

For parents and carers, it is essential to provide a supportive environment for individuals struggling with poor concentration and memory. Encouraging routine, minimizing distractions, and offering assistance with organization and memory aids can all contribute to improving cognitive functioning.

Patients must be patient with themselves and understand that poor concentration and memory are common symptoms of psychosis. Engaging in cognitive exercises, such as puzzles or memory games, can help stimulate the brain and enhance cognitive abilities over time.

It is important for the general public to be aware of the challenges faced by individuals during a psychotic breakdown. By understanding the impact of poor concentration and memory on individuals' lives, we can foster empathy and contribute to a more inclusive and supportive society.

In conclusion, poor concentration and memory are common symptoms experienced during a psychotic breakdown. Understanding the causes and seeking appropriate treatment and support are crucial for individuals, parents, and carers. By fostering empathy and awareness in the general public, we can contribute to a more understanding and inclusive society for those struggling with psychotic breakdowns.

Chapter 4: Seeking Help and Diagnosis

First Signs and Red Flags

Recognizing the early signs and red flags of a psychotic breakdown is crucial for early intervention and effective management. In this subchapter, we will explore the initial indicators that may suggest the onset of a psychotic episode, the red flags to watch out for, and the importance of seeking timely professional help.

Psychotic breakdowns are characterized by a loss of touch with reality, often accompanied by hallucinations, delusions, and disorganized thinking. However, the journey towards a full-blown psychotic episode usually begins with subtle signs that might be easy to overlook or dismiss. By being aware of these initial indicators, individuals, their loved ones, and caregivers can take proactive steps to address the situation.

One of the first signs of a potential psychotic breakdown is a gradual decline in social functioning. This may manifest as withdrawing from social activities, isolating oneself from friends and family, or struggling to maintain relationships and employment. Paying attention to such changes in behavior can help identify the need for further investigation.

Another early sign to be cautious of is a decline in overall personal hygiene and self-care. This can include neglecting grooming habits, disregarding personal appearance, and failing to maintain a clean living environment. These changes may indicate a loss of motivation and an inability to carry out daily tasks effectively.

In addition to behavioral changes, individuals may experience alterations in their thought patterns and perceptions. This could involve having unusual or irrational beliefs, feeling suspicious of others, or experiencing heightened anxiety. Other signs may include difficulties with concentration, memory lapses, and disorganized speech.

Recognizing these initial signs is crucial, but it is equally important to be aware of the red flags that indicate the need for immediate professional intervention. These red flags include a sudden and severe deterioration in mental health, an increase in suicidal thoughts or self-harm behavior, or the presence of dangerous or violent behavior towards oneself or others.

If you or someone you know is exhibiting these red flags, it is crucial to seek help promptly. Mental health professionals, such as psychiatrists, psychologists, or counselors, can provide a comprehensive evaluation, diagnosis, and personalized treatment plan. Early intervention greatly enhances the chances of successful recovery and minimizes the potential long-term impact of a psychotic breakdown.

Remember, identifying the first signs and red flags of a psychotic breakdown is the first step towards effective treatment. By understanding and being proactive, individuals, their families, and caregivers can play a vital role in supporting early intervention and promoting recovery.

Importance of Early Intervention

Title: Importance of Early Intervention: A Pathway to Recovery

Introduction:
In the realm of mental health, early intervention plays a pivotal role in addressing and managing conditions like psychotic breakdown. Recognizing the importance of timely intervention can significantly impact the overall prognosis, enabling individuals to regain control of their lives. This subchapter explores the significance of early intervention in understanding the causes, symptoms, and recovery of psychotic breakdowns.

Understanding Psychotic Breakdown:
Psychotic breakdowns are complex mental health conditions characterized by a loss of contact with reality, including hallucinations, delusions, and disorganized thinking. While the causes of psychotic breakdowns can vary, early intervention is crucial in identifying the underlying triggers and implementing appropriate treatment.

The Impact of Early Intervention:
1. Improved Outcomes: Early intervention offers the best chance for

successful treatment and recovery. By promptly addressing the symptoms and causes of psychotic breakdowns, individuals can regain stability and reduce the risk of relapse.

2. Enhanced Quality of Life: Early intervention helps individuals and their families to navigate the challenges posed by psychotic breakdowns. By providing the necessary tools, support, and resources, early intervention promotes a more fulfilling and productive life, enabling individuals to achieve their goals.

3. Reduced Stigma: Early intervention helps combat the stigma associated with mental health conditions. By raising awareness about psychotic breakdowns and their early signs, we can foster a more understanding and compassionate society.

Signs and Symptoms:
Recognizing the signs and symptoms of psychotic breakdowns is vital for early intervention. These may include sudden changes in behavior, excessive paranoia, social withdrawal, difficulty in organizing thoughts, and hallucinations. Educating the general public, patients, parents, and carers about these warning signs can encourage timely intervention.

Role of Caregivers and Support Systems:
Early intervention necessitates the active involvement of caregivers and support systems. By fostering open communication channels, providing emotional support, and connecting individuals with appropriate mental health professionals, caregivers can play a crucial role in facilitating early intervention.

Conclusion:
Early intervention is a powerful tool in the management and recovery of psychotic breakdowns. By recognizing the importance of prompt action, individuals, families, and communities can empower themselves to identify the signs, seek help, and provide supportive networks for those affected. Together, we can pave the way for a

more compassionate and understanding society that supports the mental well-being of all its members.

Diagnostic Process

The diagnostic process is a crucial step in understanding and addressing psychotic breakdowns. It involves a series of assessments, evaluations, and examinations to determine the underlying causes, symptoms, and appropriate treatment options for individuals experiencing these episodes. This subchapter will explore the diagnostic process in detail, providing insight into what patients, parents, and carers can expect when seeking help for someone going through a psychotic breakdown.

The first step in the diagnostic process is the initial evaluation, where a healthcare professional will conduct a comprehensive interview to gather information about the individual's symptoms, medical history, and any potential triggers or stressors. This interview aims to establish a preliminary understanding of the situation and determine if further assessments are required.

Once the initial evaluation is completed, additional assessments may be conducted to gain a more comprehensive understanding of the individual's mental state. These assessments can include psychological tests, neurological examinations, and laboratory tests to rule out any underlying medical conditions that may be contributing to the psychotic breakdown.

One of the key elements of the diagnostic process is the identification of specific symptoms associated with psychotic breakdowns. These symptoms can vary from person to person but often include hallucinations, delusions, disorganized thinking, and difficulties with social interactions and communication. By carefully analyzing these symptoms, healthcare professionals can make an accurate diagnosis and develop an appropriate treatment plan.

It is essential to involve not only the individual experiencing the psychotic breakdown but also their parents and carers in the diagnostic process. Their insights and observations are valuable in providing a comprehensive understanding of the individual's experiences and behaviors. Moreover, including them in the process helps establish a support network and ensures open communication channels throughout the treatment journey.

Finally, the diagnostic process should not be seen as a one-time event but rather as an ongoing assessment. Regular check-ins and evaluations are necessary to monitor progress, adjust treatment plans if needed, and ensure the individual is on the path to recovery.

Understanding the diagnostic process can alleviate some of the anxiety and uncertainty that comes with experiencing or caring for someone going through a psychotic breakdown. By actively participating in the process and maintaining open lines of communication with healthcare professionals, patients, parents, and carers can contribute towards a more accurate diagnosis and effective treatment options, leading to improved outcomes and a brighter future.

Medical Evaluation

In the journey of navigating a psychotic breakdown, one crucial step is undergoing a medical evaluation. This process plays a vital role in understanding the causes and symptoms of a psychotic breakdown, as well as determining appropriate treatment options. In this subchapter, we will explore the significance of a medical evaluation, the steps involved, and its benefits for individuals experiencing a psychotic breakdown.

A medical evaluation is a comprehensive assessment conducted by healthcare professionals to gather information about an individual's physical and mental health. This evaluation typically involves a thorough review of medical history, physical examination, and laboratory tests. For individuals experiencing a psychotic breakdown, a medical evaluation is crucial to rule out any underlying medical conditions that may be contributing to or mimicking the symptoms of psychosis.

During the evaluation, healthcare professionals may ask about symptoms such as hallucinations, delusions, disorganized thinking, and changes in behavior or mood. They may also inquire about any recent stressful events or substance use. Additionally, a physical examination may be performed to identify any physical health issues that could be causing or exacerbating psychiatric symptoms.

Laboratory tests, such as blood tests, may also be conducted to check for any abnormalities or imbalances in the body that could be affecting mental health. These tests can help determine if there are any underlying medical conditions, such as infections, hormonal imbalances, or nutritional deficiencies, which may be contributing to the psychotic breakdown.

The benefits of a medical evaluation are multifold. Firstly, it helps to establish an accurate diagnosis by ruling out other potential causes of psychosis, such as drug-induced psychosis or medical conditions like brain tumors or autoimmune disorders. Furthermore, identifying any underlying medical conditions ensures appropriate treatment and management of both the physical and mental health aspects of the individual.

Involving patients, parents, and caregivers in the medical evaluation process is essential. It allows them to actively participate in understanding the causes and contributing factors of the psychotic breakdown. This knowledge empowers them to support the individual better, advocate for their needs, and work collaboratively with healthcare professionals to develop an effective treatment plan.

In conclusion, undergoing a medical evaluation is a crucial step in the journey of navigating a psychotic breakdown. It provides valuable insights into the causes and symptoms of psychosis, helps rule out other potential medical conditions, and ensures appropriate treatment and management. By actively participating in this process, individuals, parents, and caregivers can contribute to the overall well-being and recovery of those experiencing a psychotic breakdown.

Psychological Assessment

Psychological Assessment: Understanding the Causes, Symptoms, and Recovery of Psychotic Breakdown

Psychotic breakdowns can be incredibly challenging experiences for both individuals and their loved ones. These episodes can disrupt daily life, causing confusion, fear, and distress. If you or someone you care about is going through this difficult period, understanding the importance of psychological assessment can provide valuable insights and pave the way for effective treatment options and recovery.

Psychological assessment is a comprehensive evaluation conducted by mental health professionals to gain a deeper understanding of an individual's psychological functioning. It involves a series of tests, interviews, and observations aimed at identifying the causes, symptoms, and severity of a person's psychotic breakdown. This evaluation plays a crucial role in determining the most suitable treatment approach and monitoring progress over time.

During a psychological assessment, professionals will explore various aspects of an individual's life, such as personal and medical history, family dynamics, and past traumas. They may also administer specific tests to assess cognitive abilities, mood, and overall mental health. By gathering this information, clinicians can develop a personalized treatment plan that addresses the unique needs of each individual.

For the general public, patients, parents, and carers, understanding the purpose and process of psychological assessment is essential.

Firstly, it helps to identify the underlying causes of a psychotic breakdown. While genetic factors and brain chemistry play a role, certain life events, stressors, and substance abuse can also contribute to these episodes. By pinpointing the specific triggers, individuals and their support networks can better understand the circumstances leading to the breakdown.

Secondly, psychological assessment aids in recognizing and diagnosing symptoms accurately. Symptoms of psychotic breakdowns can vary widely, including hallucinations, delusions, disorganized thinking, and social withdrawal. Through assessment, mental health professionals can determine the severity of these symptoms and develop appropriate interventions to manage and minimize their impact on daily life.

Lastly, psychological assessment provides a baseline to monitor progress and recovery. By regularly evaluating an individual's mental health, clinicians can assess the effectiveness of treatment interventions and make necessary adjustments to maximize recovery outcomes.

Navigating a psychotic breakdown can be overwhelming, but psychological assessment serves as a guiding light throughout the process. It helps individuals and their support networks gain a better understanding of the causes, symptoms, and severity of the breakdown, leading to more targeted and effective treatment options. Remember, seeking professional help and engaging in a comprehensive assessment is an essential step towards the path of recovery. With the right support and treatment, individuals can regain control of their lives and build a brighter future.

Chapter 5: Treatment Options for Psychotic Breakdown

Medication-Based Treatments

Psychotic breakdowns can be a challenging and distressing experience for individuals and their loved ones. Thankfully, there are various treatment options available to help manage and alleviate the symptoms associated with these episodes. Medication-based treatments, in particular, have proven to be effective in helping individuals regain control of their lives and facilitate a smoother recovery process.

Medication-based treatments for psychotic breakdowns primarily involve the use of antipsychotic medications. These medications work by targeting and reducing the abnormal brain activity that contributes to the development of psychotic symptoms. They can help alleviate hallucinations, delusions, and disorganized thinking, allowing individuals to regain a sense of clarity and stability.

It is essential to understand that medication-based treatments should always be prescribed and monitored by qualified healthcare professionals, such as psychiatrists or psychiatric nurse practitioners. They will evaluate the severity of symptoms, individual needs, and potential side effects to determine the most appropriate medication and dosage.

When it comes to antipsychotic medications, there are two main types: typical and atypical antipsychotics. Typical antipsychotics, such as haloperidol and chlorpromazine, have been used for many years and are effective in managing symptoms. However, they may also come with more severe side effects such as movement disorders. Atypical antipsychotics, such as risperidone and olanzapine, are newer medications that are often better tolerated and have a reduced risk of movement-related side effects.

It is important to note that medication-based treatments are not a cure for psychotic breakdowns. They are primarily aimed at managing symptoms and preventing future episodes. Alongside medication, other forms of treatment, such as therapy and support networks, are crucial in helping individuals on their path to recovery.

While medication-based treatments can be highly effective, it is essential to have open and ongoing communication with healthcare professionals. Regular check-ins and discussions about medication effectiveness and potential side effects are crucial. It is not uncommon for adjustments to be made to medication dosages or types based on individual responses.

In conclusion, medication-based treatments play a vital role in managing and alleviating the symptoms associated with psychotic breakdowns. They can provide individuals with a sense of stability, clarity, and control in their lives. However, it is important to remember that medication should always be prescribed and monitored by healthcare professionals in conjunction with other treatments to ensure the best possible outcomes for individuals experiencing psychotic breakdowns.

Antipsychotic Medications

Antipsychotic medications are a vital component of the treatment plan for individuals experiencing a psychotic breakdown. These medications, also known as neuroleptics, help manage and alleviate the distressing symptoms associated with psychosis, allowing individuals to regain control over their lives and promoting their journey towards recovery.

Psychotic breakdowns can occur for various reasons, such as genetic predisposition, environmental stressors, substance abuse, or underlying medical conditions. When someone experiences a psychotic breakdown, they may exhibit symptoms like hallucinations, delusions, disorganized thinking, and difficulty functioning in daily life. Antipsychotic medications work by targeting specific neurotransmitters in the brain, helping to restore the chemical imbalances that contribute to these symptoms.

There are two main types of antipsychotic medications: typical and atypical. Typical antipsychotics have been used since the mid-20th century and are effective in managing positive symptoms of psychosis, such as hallucinations and delusions. However, they may also cause more severe side effects, such as movement disorders. On the other hand, atypical antipsychotics are newer medications that not only alleviate positive symptoms but also help with negative symptoms like social withdrawal and lack of motivation. Atypical antipsychotics tend to have fewer movement-related side effects but can still cause weight gain and metabolic changes.

It is important to note that the decision to start antipsychotic medication should be made in consultation with a qualified healthcare professional who can assess the individual's unique needs and potential risks. The medication's dosage and duration will be tailored to each person, considering factors like age, overall health, and potential interactions with other medications.

While antipsychotic medications can significantly improve symptoms, they are not a cure for psychosis. They work hand in hand with other forms of treatment, such as therapy, social support, and lifestyle changes. It is crucial for patients, parents, and caregivers to understand that recovery from a psychotic breakdown is a gradual process that requires patience and perseverance.

In conclusion, antipsychotic medications play a crucial role in the treatment of psychotic breakdowns. These medications help manage the distressing symptoms associated with psychosis, allowing individuals to regain control over their lives and work towards recovery. However, it is essential to work closely with healthcare professionals to find the most suitable medication and dosage, as well as combine medication with other therapeutic interventions. By understanding and embracing the multifaceted nature of treatment, individuals experiencing a psychotic breakdown can navigate their way towards a brighter future.

Mood Stabilizers

In the journey of understanding and managing psychotic breakdowns, there are various treatment options available to individuals affected by this condition. One such treatment approach is the use of mood stabilizers. This subchapter aims to shed light on the role of mood stabilizers in the treatment of psychotic breakdowns, providing valuable insights for the general public, patients, parents, and caregivers.

Mood stabilizers are a class of medications primarily used to manage mood disorders, including bipolar disorder, which often accompanies psychotic breakdowns. These medications help regulate and stabilize mood swings, preventing extreme highs (mania) and lows (depression) commonly experienced by individuals with these conditions. By reducing mood fluctuations, mood stabilizers play a crucial role in managing symptoms and supporting the recovery process.

One commonly prescribed mood stabilizer is lithium. Lithium has been used for decades and is effective in managing bipolar disorder and certain types of psychosis. It helps to stabilize mood by altering neurotransmitter levels in the brain, reducing manic episodes while preventing depressive episodes. It is important to note that lithium requires careful monitoring of blood levels to ensure its effectiveness and minimize side effects.

Another frequently prescribed mood stabilizer is valproate. Valproate is effective in managing mood swings and aggression associated with bipolar disorder. It works by increasing the levels of gamma-aminobutyric acid (GABA), a neurotransmitter that helps regulate mood and behavior. However, it is essential to discuss potential risks, such as liver damage, with a healthcare professional before starting valproate.

In addition to lithium and valproate, other mood stabilizers, such as carbamazepine and lamotrigine, may also be utilized depending on the individual's specific needs and response to treatment. It is important to remember that medication selection and dosage should be determined by a qualified healthcare professional, as individual responses to different mood stabilizers may vary.

While mood stabilizers are effective in managing symptoms of bipolar disorder and related conditions, they are just one component of a comprehensive treatment plan. Psychotherapy, support from loved ones, and lifestyle modifications, such as regular exercise and healthy sleep patterns, are equally important in achieving long-term stability and recovery.

In conclusion, mood stabilizers play a crucial role in managing the mood swings and extreme fluctuations experienced by individuals with bipolar disorder and other associated conditions. Lithium, valproate, carbamazepine, and lamotrigine are commonly prescribed mood stabilizers that help regulate mood, prevent manic and depressive episodes, and support the recovery process. However, it is vital to consult with a healthcare professional to determine the most suitable medication and dosage for each individual. Together with other treatment approaches, mood stabilizers contribute to the overall well-being and stability of individuals navigating through psychotic breakdowns.

Psychotherapy Approaches

Psychotherapy approaches play a vital role in the treatment and recovery of individuals experiencing a psychotic breakdown. These therapeutic techniques aim to address the underlying causes, alleviate distressing symptoms, and empower patients to regain control over their lives. In this subchapter, we will explore some of the most effective psychotherapy approaches utilized in the treatment of psychotic breakdowns.

One widely recognized approach is cognitive-behavioral therapy (CBT). CBT helps patients identify and challenge negative thought patterns, beliefs, and behaviors that contribute to their distress. By working with a trained therapist, individuals can learn new coping strategies, develop healthier perspectives, and effectively manage the symptoms associated with psychotic breakdowns. CBT has shown promising results in reducing symptoms such as delusions, hallucinations, and paranoia.

Another valuable approach is family therapy. Psychotic breakdowns not only impact the individual but also their loved ones. Family therapy focuses on improving communication, understanding, and support within the family unit. It provides a safe space for patients, parents, and caregivers to express their concerns, learn about the condition, and work together towards the patient's recovery. Family therapy can create a network of support, reduce stress, and enhance the overall well-being of everyone involved.

Psychoeducation is another integral part of the treatment process. It involves educating patients, parents, and caregivers about the causes, symptoms, and available treatment options for psychotic breakdowns. By increasing their knowledge and understanding, individuals can actively participate in their own recovery journey, make informed decisions, and effectively manage the condition. Psychoeducation also helps reduce stigma and promotes empathy and acceptance within the community.

Furthermore, psychodynamic therapy focuses on exploring the unconscious conflicts and unresolved issues that may contribute to the development of psychotic breakdowns. By delving into the patient's personal history and experiences, psychodynamic therapy aims to provide insight, promote self-awareness, and facilitate the healing process. This approach can help individuals gain a deeper understanding of their emotions, thoughts, and behaviors, leading to long-term recovery and personal growth.

It is essential to note that different individuals may respond differently to various psychotherapy approaches, and it is crucial to find the approach that suits each patient's needs. Additionally, psychotherapy is often combined with medication to provide a comprehensive treatment plan.

In conclusion, psychotherapy approaches are invaluable tools in the treatment and recovery of individuals experiencing a psychotic breakdown. Whether it is cognitive-behavioral therapy, family therapy, psychoeducation, or psychodynamic therapy, these approaches aim to address the underlying causes, alleviate symptoms, and empower patients, parents, and caregivers. By utilizing these therapeutic techniques, individuals can reclaim their lives, foster resilience, and achieve long-term recovery.

Cognitive Behavioral Therapy (CBT)

When it comes to treating psychotic breakdowns, there is a wide range of treatment options available. One of the most effective and widely used therapies is Cognitive Behavioral Therapy (CBT). In this subchapter, we will explore what CBT is, how it can help individuals experiencing a psychotic breakdown, and its benefits for the recovery process.

CBT is a form of talk therapy that focuses on the connection between our thoughts, feelings, and behaviors. It is based on the understanding that our thoughts influence our emotions and actions, and by changing our thoughts, we can change how we feel and behave.

For individuals experiencing a psychotic breakdown, CBT can be a valuable tool in managing symptoms and promoting recovery. It helps patients gain insight into their distorted thoughts and beliefs, which are often at the root of their psychosis. By identifying and challenging these thoughts, individuals can learn to develop healthier and more realistic thinking patterns.

During CBT sessions, a therapist will work closely with the patient to explore their thoughts and beliefs, and how they are affecting their emotions and behaviors. The therapist will help the patient identify any cognitive distortions and develop strategies to replace them with more accurate and positive thoughts. This process can be empowering for patients, as it allows them to regain control over their thoughts and emotions.

CBT also equips individuals with coping skills to manage their symptoms effectively. Patients learn strategies to challenge and reframe their thoughts, develop problem-solving skills, and engage in activities that promote well-being and reduce stress. These skills can be invaluable in preventing relapses and maintaining long-term recovery.

One of the significant benefits of CBT is its collaborative nature. Patients actively participate in their treatment, working hand-in-hand with their therapist to set goals and develop coping strategies. This collaborative approach empowers patients and helps build a strong therapeutic alliance, which is crucial for successful treatment outcomes.

In conclusion, CBT is a powerful tool in the treatment of psychotic breakdowns. By addressing the connection between thoughts, emotions, and behaviors, it helps individuals gain insight into their distorted thinking patterns and equips them with coping skills for managing symptoms. CBT fosters a collaborative therapeutic relationship and empowers patients to take an active role in their recovery journey. If you or someone you know is experiencing a psychotic breakdown, exploring the benefits of CBT with a qualified therapist may be a step towards healing and regaining control over one's life.

Family Therapy

Family Therapy is an essential component in the treatment of individuals experiencing a psychotic breakdown. This subchapter aims to shed light on the significance of involving the entire family unit in the recovery process. By addressing the causes, symptoms, and recovery options related to psychotic breakdowns, it is crucial to recognize the impact that family dynamics can have on an individual's mental health journey.

Psychotic breakdowns can be incredibly challenging for both the individual experiencing them and their loved ones. It is during these times that the support and understanding of family members become paramount. Family therapy provides a safe and structured environment for open communication, fostering empathy, and promoting healing for everyone involved.

One of the primary goals of family therapy in relation to psychotic breakdowns is to educate family members about the causes and symptoms of these episodes. By providing a comprehensive understanding of the condition, families can better comprehend their loved one's experiences and avoid misconceptions or stigmatization. Understanding that psychotic breakdowns are not the result of personal weakness or character flaws, but rather a complex interplay of genetic, environmental, and psychological factors, is crucial for family members to offer appropriate support.

Furthermore, family therapy helps in identifying and addressing any dysfunctional patterns or dynamics within the family system that may contribute to the individual's vulnerability to psychotic breakdowns. Through guided discussions and interventions, family members can explore their roles, communication styles, and unresolved conflicts that may impact the overall mental well-being of their loved one.

Family therapy also plays a vital role in the recovery process by providing a support network for the individual experiencing the psychotic breakdown. When family members actively participate in therapy, they learn strategies to assist their loved one in managing their symptoms, such as recognizing early warning signs, promoting medication adherence, and implementing healthy coping mechanisms.

In summary, family therapy is an invaluable resource for individuals and their families navigating through the challenges of psychotic breakdowns. By fostering understanding, providing support, and addressing dysfunctional dynamics, family therapy contributes significantly to the overall recovery process. It empowers families to become active participants in their loved one's journey towards mental health and promotes a nurturing environment for long-term stability and well-being.

Alternative and Complementary Treatments

When it comes to treating psychotic breakdowns, traditional medications and therapy are often the first line of defense. However, some individuals may seek alternative and complementary treatments to augment their recovery process. It is important to note that while these treatments may have potential benefits, they should always be used in conjunction with, and not as a replacement for, evidence-based medical interventions.

One popular alternative treatment for psychotic breakdowns is acupuncture. This ancient Chinese practice involves the insertion of thin needles into specific points on the body to promote healing and balance. Advocates of acupuncture believe that it can help alleviate symptoms such as anxiety, depression, and even hallucinations. While research on this topic is limited, some individuals report positive effects from acupuncture sessions, often noting improved overall well-being and reduced stress levels.

Another complementary treatment that has gained attention in recent years is mindfulness meditation. This practice involves focusing one's attention on the present moment, cultivating awareness, and accepting one's experiences without judgment. Mindfulness meditation has been shown to reduce stress, improve sleep, and enhance overall mental well-being. While it may not directly address the underlying causes of a psychotic breakdown, it can serve as a valuable tool in managing symptoms and promoting a sense of calmness and clarity.

Additionally, certain nutritional supplements are believed to have potential benefits for individuals experiencing psychotic breakdowns. For example, omega-3 fatty acids found in fish oil have been studied for their potential to reduce symptoms of psychosis. Similarly, certain vitamins, such as B-complex vitamins and vitamin D, have been explored for their potential role in supporting mental health. However, it is important to consult with a healthcare professional before starting any new supplements, as they can interact with medications or have unintended side effects.

It is crucial to approach alternative and complementary treatments with an open mind and a critical eye. While some individuals may find these treatments helpful, others may not experience the same benefits. It is essential to remember that everyone's journey to recovery is unique, and what works for one person may not work for another.

In conclusion, alternative and complementary treatments can serve as valuable additions to traditional medical interventions for individuals experiencing a psychotic breakdown. Acupuncture, mindfulness meditation, and certain nutritional supplements are just a few examples of these treatments. However, it is important to approach these options with caution and consult with healthcare professionals before incorporating them into a treatment plan. Ultimately, the goal is to find a comprehensive approach that addresses the underlying causes of the psychotic breakdown and supports the individual's overall well-being.

Art Therapy

Art therapy is a powerful and effective tool that can play a significant role in the treatment and recovery of individuals experiencing a psychotic breakdown. It harnesses the healing power of art to help individuals express their thoughts, emotions, and experiences in a non-verbal and creative manner. This subchapter explores the benefits, techniques, and applications of art therapy in the context of psychotic breakdown.

Art therapy offers a safe and non-threatening space for individuals to explore their inner world and communicate their feelings and experiences that may be difficult to put into words. Through various art forms, such as painting, drawing, sculpture, and collage, individuals can express their struggles, fears, and hopes, providing valuable insights for both themselves and their therapists.

One of the significant benefits of art therapy is its ability to provide a sense of control and empowerment to individuals during a psychotic breakdown. Engaging in the creative process allows individuals to take charge of their narratives, providing a sense of agency and self-expression. This can be particularly empowering for patients who may feel overwhelmed by their symptoms or disconnected from their sense of self.

Art therapy also facilitates a deeper understanding and processing of emotions and experiences. By externalizing internal struggles through art, individuals can gain a fresh perspective on their feelings and experiences. This process can lead to increased self-awareness, insight, and a greater capacity to cope with the challenges of a psychotic breakdown.

Furthermore, art therapy can foster a sense of connection and support within a therapeutic setting. Group art therapy sessions allow individuals to share their artwork and stories with others who may be going through similar experiences. This sense of community and shared understanding can help reduce feelings of isolation and provide a valuable support network during the recovery process.

In conclusion, art therapy is an invaluable tool in the treatment and recovery of individuals experiencing a psychotic breakdown. By providing a creative outlet for self-expression, empowerment, and insight, it can facilitate healing and growth. Whether you are a patient, parent, carer, or a general reader interested in understanding psychotic breakdown and its treatment options, exploring art therapy as part of the recovery journey can offer a unique and beneficial approach to healing.

Yoga and Mindfulness Practices

Yoga and Mindfulness Practices: Enhancing Recovery and Well-being

In recent years, the role of complementary and alternative therapies in mental health care has gained significant attention. Among these approaches, yoga and mindfulness practices have emerged as powerful tools for promoting well-being and aiding in the recovery process for individuals experiencing a psychotic breakdown. This subchapter explores the benefits of incorporating yoga and mindfulness practices into the treatment and management of psychotic breakdown, shedding light on how these practices can positively impact individuals, their families, and their caregivers.

Yoga, a mind-body practice originating from ancient India, combines physical postures, breathing techniques, and meditation to promote relaxation, flexibility, and overall physical and mental health. Mindfulness, on the other hand, involves intentionally paying attention to the present moment, without judgment. Both practices have been extensively studied and proven to reduce stress, anxiety, and depression, while improving overall mental well-being.

For individuals experiencing a psychotic breakdown, yoga and mindfulness practices offer a unique set of benefits. By incorporating these practices into their daily routines, patients can develop increased self-awareness, emotional regulation, and a sense of empowerment. Yoga can help individuals reconnect with their bodies, promoting a sense of grounding and stability during episodes of psychosis. Similarly, mindfulness practices can help patients cultivate non-reactivity to distressing thoughts and emotions, allowing them to observe their experiences without becoming overwhelmed.

Furthermore, yoga and mindfulness practices can also benefit the parents, carers, and families of individuals going through a psychotic breakdown. These practices can provide them with stress reduction techniques, improve their own self-care, and enhance their ability to support their loved ones. By incorporating mindfulness and yoga into their daily lives, parents and carers can develop a greater sense of patience, compassion, and understanding, which are crucial in effectively assisting someone through their recovery journey.

It is important to note that yoga and mindfulness practices should not replace traditional treatment options for psychotic breakdowns, such as medication and therapy. Instead, they should be seen as complementary tools that can enhance overall well-being and aid in the recovery process. It is recommended that individuals consult with their healthcare providers before incorporating these practices into their treatment plan.

In conclusion, yoga and mindfulness practices have the potential to significantly contribute to the management and recovery of individuals experiencing a psychotic breakdown. By incorporating these practices into their daily routines, patients, parents, and carers can experience enhanced well-being, increased self-awareness, and improved emotional regulation. As part of a holistic approach to treatment, yoga and mindfulness practices offer valuable tools for navigating the challenges of psychotic breakdowns and promoting long-term recovery.

Chapter 6: Recovery and Rehabilitation

Understanding the Recovery Process

Recovering from a psychotic breakdown can be a challenging and complex journey, but it is important to remember that there is hope and support available. This subchapter aims to shed light on the recovery process, providing guidance and understanding for individuals experiencing a psychotic breakdown, as well as their loved ones and caregivers.

Recovery from a psychotic breakdown involves various stages, each with its own unique challenges and goals. The first step is recognizing the signs and symptoms of a psychotic episode, which may include hallucinations, delusions, disorganized thinking, and difficulty functioning in daily life. It is crucial to seek professional help as soon as possible to receive an accurate diagnosis and appropriate treatment.

Once treatment begins, individuals will often undergo a combination of medication, therapy, and other interventions tailored to their specific needs. Medications, such as antipsychotics, can help manage symptoms and stabilize mood, while therapy, such as cognitive-behavioral therapy (CBT), can assist in challenging and reshaping irrational thoughts and behaviors.

Recovery also involves developing coping strategies and support networks. Learning to identify triggers and implement self-care techniques, such as exercise, mindfulness, and stress management, can greatly contribute to the recovery process. It is equally important to surround oneself with a supportive network of family, friends, and mental health professionals who can offer understanding, encouragement, and practical assistance.

Patience and persistence are key during the recovery journey. It is not uncommon for setbacks or relapses to occur, but these should not be seen as failures. Instead, they should be viewed as opportunities for growth and learning. It is important to remember that recovery is a gradual process, and every individual's experience will be unique.

Furthermore, education and awareness play a crucial role in the recovery process. Understanding the causes and symptoms of psychotic breakdowns can help individuals and their caregivers develop a proactive approach to managing their condition. By staying informed about treatment options, new research, and community resources, individuals can make informed decisions about their recovery journey.

In conclusion, understanding the recovery process is essential for individuals experiencing a psychotic breakdown, as well as their loved ones and caregivers. Recovery involves recognizing the signs, seeking appropriate treatment, developing coping strategies, building support networks, and embracing patience and persistence. By arming oneself with knowledge and support, individuals can navigate the challenges of recovery with hope and resilience.

Rehabilitation Programs and Services

Psychotic breakdowns can be overwhelming and disruptive, affecting not only the individuals experiencing them but also their loved ones. However, it is essential to remember that recovery is possible. To support individuals in their journey towards recovery, there are various rehabilitation programs and services available.

Rehabilitation programs are designed to help individuals regain control over their lives and enhance their overall well-being. These programs offer a comprehensive approach that addresses both the physical and psychological aspects of recovery. They aim to equip individuals with the necessary tools and skills to manage their symptoms, improve their daily functioning, and reintegrate into society.

One key component of rehabilitation programs is psychoeducation. This involves providing individuals and their families with information about psychotic breakdowns, including the causes, symptoms, and treatment options. Understanding the condition can help alleviate fear and confusion, enabling individuals to actively participate in their recovery process.

Psychosocial interventions are another vital aspect of rehabilitation programs. These interventions focus on enhancing social and interpersonal skills, as well as promoting independence and self-care. They may include individual counseling, group therapy, vocational training, and support with daily living activities. By addressing these areas, individuals can regain confidence and rebuild their lives.

Medication management is often an integral part of rehabilitation programs, as medication can play a significant role in managing symptoms and preventing future psychotic episodes. A team of healthcare professionals, including psychiatrists and nurses, work closely with individuals to find the most effective medication regimen while minimizing side effects. Regular monitoring and follow-up appointments ensure that the medication remains appropriate and adjustments can be made if needed.

Community support services are also essential in the rehabilitation process. These services provide a network of support for individuals as they navigate their recovery journey. They may include support groups, peer mentoring programs, and outreach services. Connecting with others who have experienced similar challenges can provide a sense of belonging and understanding, reducing feelings of isolation.

In conclusion, rehabilitation programs and services form a crucial part of the recovery process for individuals experiencing psychotic breakdowns. By offering psychoeducation, psychosocial interventions, medication management, and community support, these programs aim to empower individuals and their families, facilitating their journey towards a meaningful and fulfilling life. If you or a loved one is going through a psychotic breakdown, reaching out to these resources can pave the way for a brighter future. Remember, recovery is possible, and support is available.

Psychosocial Rehabilitation

Psychosocial Rehabilitation: Enhancing Recovery and Rebuilding Lives

Recovering from a psychotic breakdown can be a challenging journey, not just for the individual experiencing it but also for their loved ones. The road to recovery involves not only addressing the symptoms and causes of the breakdown but also rebuilding one's life and navigating the psychosocial aspects of the condition. In this subchapter, we will explore the importance of psychosocial rehabilitation in the recovery process and provide valuable insights for patients, parents, and carers.

Psychosocial rehabilitation focuses on restoring an individual's ability to function in their daily lives, fostering independence, and improving their overall well-being. It recognizes that mental health recovery is not solely about managing symptoms, but also about rebuilding social connections, developing coping skills, and reclaiming a meaningful life.

One of the key components of psychosocial rehabilitation is the creation of a supportive and inclusive environment. Patients, parents, and carers play a vital role in facilitating this process by offering understanding, empathy, and support. By educating themselves about the symptoms and causes of psychotic breakdown, they can provide a safe space for open communication and encourage the individual to seek appropriate treatment.

Recovery-oriented interventions, such as cognitive-behavioral therapy and skills training, are also essential in psychosocial rehabilitation. These interventions aim to enhance coping skills, improve problem-solving abilities, and promote positive self-identity. Patients can learn to challenge negative thoughts, manage stress, and develop strategies to cope with daily challenges. Parents and carers can support this process by actively participating in therapy sessions, encouraging the practice of learned skills, and providing a nurturing environment.

Another crucial aspect of psychosocial rehabilitation is community integration. Support groups, vocational training, and social activities can help individuals rebuild their social networks, regain a sense of purpose, and engage in meaningful occupations. Encouraging participation in community events, hobbies, and volunteering can foster a sense of belonging and provide valuable opportunities for personal growth.

Psychosocial rehabilitation is an ongoing process that requires patience and perseverance. It is important to remember that recovery is a unique journey for each individual, and progress may vary. By embracing the principles of psychosocial rehabilitation, patients, parents, and carers can work together to enhance recovery, rebuild lives, and foster a supportive environment for long-term well-being.

In conclusion, psychosocial rehabilitation is an integral part of the recovery process for individuals experiencing a psychotic breakdown. By focusing on rebuilding lives, developing coping skills, and fostering community integration, this approach can help individuals regain their independence and improve their overall quality of life. With the support of their loved ones, patients can navigate the challenges of recovery and find the strength to overcome the impact of a psychotic breakdown.

Vocational Training and Support

When individuals experience a psychotic breakdown, it can deeply impact their ability to function in various aspects of life, including work and career aspirations. However, it is important to remember that with the right support and vocational training, individuals can regain control over their lives and even pursue fulfilling careers. This subchapter explores the importance of vocational training and support in the recovery process, addressing the needs of the general public, patients, parents, and carers.

Vocational training serves as a crucial component of recovery for individuals who have experienced a psychotic breakdown. It focuses on building skills, developing self-confidence, and fostering independence. Through vocational training programs, individuals can acquire job-specific skills, learn effective communication techniques, and enhance their problem-solving abilities. These programs often offer a supportive environment where individuals can practice their newfound skills and receive feedback from experienced professionals.

One of the primary goals of vocational training is to help individuals find meaningful employment. It is essential to recognize that recovery from a psychotic breakdown does not necessarily mean returning to the same job or career path. Vocational training can assist individuals in identifying their strengths, interests, and goals, enabling them to explore new career possibilities that align with their current abilities and aspirations. By doing so, individuals can regain a sense of purpose and fulfillment in their professional lives.

In addition to vocational training, ongoing support is vital for individuals during their recovery journey. Support networks, such as support groups, peer mentors, and vocational rehabilitation services, play a crucial role in providing guidance, encouragement, and assistance. These resources help individuals navigate the challenges they may encounter while pursuing employment, such as managing symptoms, disclosing their condition to employers, and adapting to workplace dynamics.

Furthermore, parents and carers play a pivotal role in supporting individuals during their vocational training and beyond. By offering emotional support, understanding, and advocacy, parents and carers can empower individuals to pursue their career goals and overcome any obstacles they may face.

In conclusion, vocational training and support are integral components of the recovery process for individuals who have experienced a psychotic breakdown. Through vocational training, individuals can acquire job-specific skills, explore new career possibilities, and regain a sense of purpose. Ongoing support, including support networks and the involvement of parents and carers, is crucial in helping individuals navigate the challenges of the employment journey. By providing vocational training and support, we can empower individuals to rebuild their lives, achieve their career aspirations, and thrive in their chosen fields.

Strategies for Successful Recovery

Recovering from a psychotic breakdown can be a challenging and overwhelming journey, but with the right strategies, it is possible to regain control over your life and find the path to wellness. In this subchapter, we will explore some effective strategies for successful recovery that can be applied by individuals experiencing a psychotic breakdown, as well as their loved ones.

1. Education and Understanding: Knowledge is power when it comes to managing a psychotic breakdown. Educating yourself, as well as your support system, about the causes, symptoms, and treatment options is crucial. Understanding the nature of psychosis will help you navigate through the recovery process more confidently.

2. Seek Professional Help: It is essential to reach out to mental health professionals who specialize in treating psychotic disorders. Psychologists, psychiatrists, and therapists can provide the necessary guidance, support, and evidence-based treatments to aid your recovery.

3. Medication Compliance: Medication plays a vital role in managing psychotic symptoms. Adhering to prescribed medications, attending regular appointments with your mental health professional, and openly discussing any concerns or side effects can significantly contribute to your recovery.

4. Psychotherapy and Counseling: Alongside medication, psychotherapy and counseling can be invaluable tools for recovery. Cognitive-behavioral therapy (CBT) and family therapy have shown great promise in helping individuals and their families understand and cope with the challenges posed by psychosis.

5. Building a Support Network: Surrounding yourself with a strong support network can make a significant difference in your recovery journey. Connecting with individuals who have experienced similar challenges, joining support groups, and involving loved ones in your treatment can provide the emotional support you need.

6. Self-Care and Stress Management: Prioritizing self-care activities such as exercise, proper nutrition, adequate sleep, and stress reduction techniques can enhance your overall well-being and aid in your recovery. Engaging in activities you enjoy and finding healthy outlets for stress can also contribute to your overall stability.

7. Setting Realistic Goals: It is important to set achievable goals during your recovery process. Breaking down larger goals into smaller, manageable steps can help you stay motivated and track your progress, ultimately leading to greater success.

Remember, recovery is a unique and personal journey, and it may take time. Be patient with yourself and celebrate even the smallest victories along the way. By implementing these strategies and working closely with your healthcare team, you can navigate the challenges of a psychotic breakdown and achieve a successful recovery.

Building a Support Network

When faced with a psychotic breakdown, it is crucial to build a strong support network to help you navigate through the challenges ahead. A support network consists of individuals who can offer emotional support, guidance, and practical assistance during your journey to recovery. This subchapter aims to provide insights into the importance of building a support network and offers strategies to cultivate one.

First and foremost, it is important to understand that you are not alone. Psychotic breakdowns can be overwhelming, but reaching out to others can alleviate some of the burdens. Your support network should include family members, friends, healthcare professionals, and support groups. These individuals can provide empathetic listening, offer encouragement, and help you access the resources you need.

Family members play a critical role in the support network, as they can offer unconditional love and understanding. They may not fully comprehend the experience of a psychotic breakdown, but open communication and education can bridge this gap. Encourage them to educate themselves about the symptoms, causes, and treatment options, so they can provide the best possible support.

Friends can also be valuable sources of support. Inform them about your situation and educate them about psychosis. True friends will stand by you, offering companionship and a listening ear. Additionally, consider joining support groups specifically tailored to individuals experiencing psychotic breakdowns. These groups provide a safe space to share your experiences, learn from others, and develop coping strategies.

Healthcare professionals are vital members of your support network. They can provide medical guidance, prescribe appropriate medications, and offer therapy options. Building a trusting relationship with your healthcare team is crucial, as they will be your allies on the path to recovery.

Lastly, self-care should not be overlooked. Engaging in activities that bring you joy and relaxation can strengthen your support network from within. Exercise, meditation, and pursuing hobbies can help you manage stress, improve your overall well-being, and increase your resilience.

In conclusion, building a support network is essential when navigating a psychotic breakdown. By reaching out to loved ones, healthcare professionals, and support groups, you can find the strength and resources needed to overcome challenges. Remember, you are not alone in this journey, and with the support of others, recovery is possible.

Managing Stress and Triggers

Stress and triggers play a significant role in the onset and exacerbation of psychotic breakdowns. Understanding how to effectively manage stress and identify triggers can greatly enhance the recovery process. In this subchapter, we will explore practical strategies to help individuals, their families, and caregivers navigate the challenges associated with stress and triggers.

Stress is an inevitable part of life, but when it becomes overwhelming, it can have detrimental effects on mental health. For individuals experiencing or recovering from a psychotic breakdown, stress can be particularly challenging. It is crucial to develop healthy coping mechanisms to reduce stress levels and prevent future episodes.

One effective method for managing stress is mindfulness meditation. This practice involves focusing on the present moment, without judgment or attachment. Mindfulness can help individuals become aware of their thoughts and emotions, allowing them to respond rather than react to stressors. Engaging in regular exercise, maintaining a balanced diet, and getting enough sleep are also essential for stress management.

Identifying triggers is another crucial aspect of managing psychotic breakdowns. Triggers are events, situations, or stimuli that can lead to the worsening of symptoms or even a full-blown relapse. By recognizing and avoiding triggers, individuals can take proactive steps to prevent episodes or minimize their impact.

Keeping a trigger journal can be immensely helpful in this process. By documenting experiences, emotions, and potential triggers, patterns may emerge, enabling individuals to anticipate and prepare for challenging situations. It is equally important for family members, caregivers, and healthcare professionals to be aware of these triggers to provide the necessary support and help create a safe environment.

In addition to avoiding triggers, developing coping strategies is vital. These strategies can include engaging in activities that promote relaxation and self-care, such as engaging in hobbies, spending time in nature, or practicing deep breathing exercises. It is essential to find what works best for each individual, as everyone's triggers and coping mechanisms may vary.

Lastly, seeking support from mental health professionals, support groups, and loved ones is crucial in managing stress and triggers. Building a strong support network can provide individuals with the resources and encouragement needed to navigate the challenges of recovery.

In conclusion, managing stress and triggers is an essential component of the recovery process for individuals experiencing or recovering from a psychotic breakdown. By implementing mindfulness techniques, identifying triggers, developing coping strategies, and seeking support, individuals can empower themselves to take control of their mental health journey. Remember, recovery is possible, and with the right tools, stress and triggers can be effectively managed, leading to a brighter and more fulfilling future.

Chapter 7: Supporting Loved Ones with Psychotic Breakdown

Understanding and Educating Yourself

When faced with the overwhelming experience of a psychotic breakdown, it is crucial to seek understanding and educate yourself about the causes, symptoms, and recovery options. This subchapter aims to provide valuable insights and information to the general public, patients, parents, and carers, helping them navigate through this challenging journey.

Understanding the causes of a psychotic breakdown is the first step towards healing. While the exact triggers can vary from person to person, factors such as genetic predisposition, environmental stressors, substance abuse, and brain chemistry imbalances can contribute to the onset of psychosis. By understanding these underlying causes, individuals and their support networks can gain a clearer perspective on the condition, reducing stigma and fostering empathy.

Recognizing the symptoms of a psychotic breakdown is crucial for early intervention and treatment. Symptoms may include hallucinations, delusions, disorganized thinking, social withdrawal, erratic behavior, and emotional instability. By familiarizing themselves with these warning signs, individuals and their loved ones can take appropriate action, seeking professional help and support as soon as possible.

Educating oneself and others about the available treatment options is essential for recovery. Psychotic breakdowns can be treated through a combination of medication, therapy, and support networks. Medications, such as antipsychotics, can help manage symptoms and stabilize brain chemistry. Therapy, including cognitive-behavioral therapy (CBT) and family therapy, can assist in developing coping strategies, understanding triggers, and rebuilding relationships.

Support networks, such as support groups and peer counseling, can provide solace and guidance throughout the recovery process.

Additionally, educating oneself about the potential challenges and experiences faced by individuals during psychosis and recovery can help foster empathy and understanding. By learning about personal accounts, success stories, and coping mechanisms shared by individuals who have navigated similar journeys, patients, parents, and carers can gain valuable insights and practical advice.

Remember, understanding and educating yourself about the causes, symptoms, and recovery options surrounding a psychotic breakdown is crucial for informed decision-making and effective support. By actively seeking knowledge and fostering empathy, individuals and their support networks can empower themselves to navigate this challenging path towards healing and recovery.

Communication Strategies

Effective communication is essential when it comes to understanding and supporting individuals experiencing a psychotic breakdown. Whether you are a patient, a parent, a caregiver, or a member of the general public, learning about communication strategies can greatly contribute to the well-being and recovery of those affected by this condition.

One of the most important aspects of communication is active listening. When engaging in a conversation with someone going through a psychotic breakdown, it is crucial to give them your full attention and show genuine interest in what they are saying. Avoid interrupting or dismissing their experiences, as this can further isolate and distress them. Instead, encourage them to express their thoughts and feelings, and validate their emotions by acknowledging their experiences.

Another effective strategy is to use simple and clear language. People experiencing a psychotic breakdown may struggle with concentration and processing information, so it is important to communicate in a straightforward and understandable manner. Avoid using jargon or complex terms, as this may confuse or overwhelm them. Instead, break down information into smaller, manageable chunks and repeat key points if necessary.

Non-verbal communication is also vital when interacting with individuals in a psychotic state. Pay attention to your body language and facial expressions, as they can convey understanding and empathy. Maintain an open and non-threatening posture, and use gentle and calm tones when speaking. This can help create a safe and supportive environment for communication.

Furthermore, it is crucial to be patient and empathetic. Psychotic breakdowns can be distressing for both the individual experiencing them and those around them. It is important to remember that their behavior and thoughts may be influenced by their condition, and not a reflection of their true personality. Show compassion and understanding, and avoid judgment or criticism. By being patient and empathetic, you can foster trust and strengthen your relationship with the person.

Lastly, seeking professional help and guidance is essential. Psychotic breakdowns require specialized treatment and support. Encourage individuals experiencing symptoms to consult a healthcare professional who can provide the appropriate interventions and therapies. Additionally, educate yourself about the causes, symptoms, and recovery options related to psychotic breakdowns. This knowledge will enable you to better understand and support the affected individuals, as well as connect them with the resources they need.

In conclusion, effective communication strategies play a crucial role in supporting individuals experiencing a psychotic breakdown. By actively listening, using simple language, employing non-verbal cues, being patient and empathetic, and seeking professional help, we can create a supportive and understanding environment for those affected by this condition. Together, we can contribute to their recovery and well-being.

Self-Care for Caregivers

Caring for someone experiencing a psychotic breakdown can be an emotionally and physically demanding task. As a caregiver, it is essential to prioritize your own well-being to provide the best support possible. This subchapter will discuss the importance of self-care and provide practical strategies to help you navigate this challenging role.

One of the first steps in self-care is acknowledging your own needs. Remember that you are also human and require attention, rest, and relaxation. Neglecting your well-being can lead to burnout and ultimately hamper your ability to provide effective care. Recognize that your role as a caregiver is crucial, and taking care of yourself does not mean neglecting your loved one.

One way to practice self-care is by setting realistic expectations. Understand that you cannot fix everything or control the outcome. Accepting this can alleviate unnecessary stress and allow you to focus on what you can do to support your loved one. Seek support from other caregivers who can relate to your experiences and offer guidance. Support groups or online communities can be an invaluable resource.

Another crucial aspect of self-care is maintaining healthy boundaries. Set limits on your time and energy to prevent feeling overwhelmed. It's okay to say no to certain tasks or delegate responsibilities to others when necessary. Remember that you are not alone in this journey, and reaching out for help is not a sign of weakness but strength.

Finding time for self-care activities is vital for your mental and physical health. Engaging in activities that bring you joy and relaxation can significantly reduce stress levels. Whether it's practicing meditation, exercising, reading a book, or pursuing a hobby, make sure to schedule regular breaks for yourself.

Additionally, taking care of your physical health is equally important. Ensure you are getting adequate sleep, eating balanced meals, and staying hydrated. These simple yet often overlooked aspects can significantly impact your ability to cope with the demands of caregiving.

Lastly, do not hesitate to seek professional help if you find yourself overwhelmed or struggling with your own mental well-being. Therapists or counselors can provide valuable guidance and support tailored to your specific needs.

Remember, self-care is not selfish; it is a necessary component of being an effective caregiver. By prioritizing your well-being, you are better equipped to provide the love, support, and care your loved one needs during their journey towards recovery.

Navigating Psychotic Breakdown: Symptoms, Causes, and Treatment Options offers essential insights into understanding and managing psychotic breakdowns. This subchapter on self-care for caregivers aims to empower the general public, patients, parents, and carers, highlighting the significance of self-care and providing practical strategies to navigate the challenges associated with caring for someone experiencing a psychotic breakdown.

Chapter 8: Promoting Mental Health and Prevention

Early Intervention and Prevention Programs

In recent years, there has been a growing recognition of the importance of early intervention and prevention programs when it comes to addressing psychotic breakdowns. These programs have proved to be invaluable in helping individuals at risk of or experiencing a psychotic episode, as well as their families and caregivers. By identifying warning signs, providing education, and offering support, these initiatives are playing a crucial role in reducing the impact of psychotic breakdowns and promoting recovery.

One of the key aspects of early intervention programs is the identification of early warning signs. These signs may include changes in behavior, social withdrawal, increased anxiety, difficulty concentrating, or unusual beliefs and perceptions. By being aware of these indicators, individuals and their loved ones can seek help early on, potentially preventing the onset or worsening of a psychotic episode. It is important for everyone to understand that seeking help promptly is not a sign of weakness but rather a proactive step towards effective treatment.

Education is another vital component of early intervention and prevention programs. By providing information about the causes, symptoms, and treatment options for psychotic breakdowns, these programs empower individuals and their families to make informed decisions. Understanding the nature of the condition can help reduce stigma and increase empathy, fostering a supportive environment for those affected by psychotic breakdowns.

Support is also a crucial element of these programs. This support can come in various forms, such as counseling, therapy, or peer support groups. By offering a safe space to discuss fears, concerns, and experiences, individuals and their families can access the emotional and practical assistance they need during difficult times. Additionally, support programs can also provide practical tools and strategies to manage symptoms and improve overall well-being.

Early intervention and prevention programs have shown promising results in terms of reducing the severity and duration of psychotic episodes. They have also been instrumental in facilitating recovery and improving long-term outcomes. However, it is essential to remember that these programs are most effective when implemented in conjunction with professional medical treatment. It is always advisable to seek the guidance of a healthcare provider or mental health professional for an accurate diagnosis and personalized treatment plan.

By investing in early intervention and prevention programs, we can empower individuals, their families, and caregivers to navigate the challenges associated with psychotic breakdowns. Together, we can create a society that supports and understands the complexities of mental health, fostering recovery and resilience for all.

Reducing Stigma and Increasing Awareness

In a world where mental health is often misunderstood, reducing the stigma surrounding psychotic breakdowns is crucial for the well-being and recovery of individuals experiencing this challenging condition. This subchapter aims to shed light on the causes, symptoms, and treatment options of psychotic breakdowns while emphasizing the importance of increasing awareness and understanding within society.

Psychotic breakdowns can affect anyone, regardless of age, gender, or background. However, the lack of understanding and empathy often leads to stigmatization and discrimination against those experiencing such episodes. It is essential for the general public, patients, parents, and carers to come together and work towards reducing this stigma, creating a more supportive environment for those struggling with psychotic breakdowns.

One of the most effective ways to reduce stigma is through education and awareness. By providing accurate information about the causes and symptoms of psychotic breakdowns, we can dispel myths and misconceptions surrounding this condition. This includes addressing the role of genetics, environmental factors, and substance abuse in triggering these episodes. By understanding that psychotic breakdowns are not a result of personal weakness or character flaws, but rather a complex interplay of biological and environmental factors, we can foster empathy and support.

Increasing awareness also involves highlighting the available treatment options and emphasizing the importance of seeking professional help. Many individuals experiencing psychotic breakdowns are fearful or hesitant to reach out for assistance due to the stigma attached to mental health issues. By stressing the effectiveness of various therapies, medication, and support systems, we can encourage early intervention, leading to better outcomes and faster recovery.

Through sharing personal stories and experiences, we can humanize the condition and help the general public, patients, parents, and carers understand the challenges faced by individuals during a psychotic breakdown. By acknowledging the courage and resilience of those who have faced and overcome this condition, we can empower others to seek help and create a more inclusive society.

To further reduce stigma and increase awareness, it is essential for healthcare professionals, policymakers, and community organizations to collaborate. By working together, we can develop targeted campaigns, educational programs, and support networks that promote understanding and empathy for individuals experiencing psychotic breakdowns.

In conclusion, reducing stigma and increasing awareness surrounding psychotic breakdowns is vital for supporting individuals through their recovery journey. By educating the general public, patients, parents, and carers about the causes, symptoms, and treatment options, we can foster empathy, understanding, and a more inclusive society. It is time to break the silence and start a dialogue that will ultimately lead to better support and improved outcomes for those impacted by psychotic breakdowns.

Lifestyle Factors for Mental Well-being

In our journey towards understanding and navigating psychotic breakdowns, it is crucial to explore the various lifestyle factors that can impact our mental well-being. While there are many causes and symptoms associated with psychotic breakdowns, incorporating positive lifestyle choices can play a significant role in promoting recovery and overall mental health. This subchapter aims to shed light on the lifestyle factors that can contribute to mental well-being, providing guidance for the general public, patients, parents, and carers.

One of the fundamental lifestyle factors for mental well-being is maintaining a healthy diet. Consuming a balanced diet rich in fruits, vegetables, whole grains, and lean proteins can provide the essential nutrients needed for brain function. Additionally, avoiding excessive caffeine, alcohol, and processed foods can help stabilize mood and reduce anxiety.

Regular physical activity is another crucial aspect of promoting mental well-being. Engaging in exercise releases endorphins, which are known to boost mood and reduce symptoms of stress and anxiety. Whether it's walking, jogging, or practicing yoga, finding an activity that you enjoy and can incorporate into your daily routine can have a positive impact on your mental health.

Adequate sleep is often underestimated but plays a vital role in maintaining mental well-being. Establishing a consistent sleep schedule and creating a relaxing bedtime routine can help ensure quality sleep. Sleep deprivation can exacerbate symptoms associated with psychotic breakdowns, so it is important to prioritize getting enough rest.

Another lifestyle factor that cannot be overlooked is the importance of social connections. Engaging in meaningful relationships, whether with friends, family, or support groups, can provide a sense of belonging, reduce feelings of isolation, and provide a support system during difficult times. Connecting with others who have gone through similar experiences can be particularly valuable for patients, parents, and carers.

Lastly, managing stress is paramount for mental well-being. Incorporating stress-reducing techniques such as meditation, deep breathing exercises, and mindfulness practices can help alleviate symptoms associated with psychotic breakdowns. It is also essential to create a healthy work-life balance and prioritize self-care activities that bring joy and relaxation.

By understanding and implementing these lifestyle factors, individuals can take an active role in promoting their own mental well-being and supporting the recovery process. Whether you are a patient, parent, carer, or a concerned member of the general public, incorporating these lifestyle choices can make a significant difference in navigating and overcoming psychotic breakdowns. Remember, small changes can lead to significant improvements in mental health, and every step towards well-being is a step in the right direction.

Chapter 9: Frequently Asked Questions (FAQs)

What is the difference between psychosis and psychotic breakdown?

Understanding the distinction between psychosis and a psychotic breakdown is crucial for those seeking to navigate the complex world of mental health. While these terms are often used interchangeably, they actually refer to different aspects of the same phenomenon. In this subchapter, we will delve into the differences between psychosis and psychotic breakdown, shedding light on their causes, symptoms, and potential paths to recovery.

Psychosis is a broad term used to describe a mental state characterized by a loss of touch with reality. It is not a diagnosis in itself but rather a symptom of an underlying mental disorder. Psychosis can manifest in various forms, such as hallucinations, delusions, disorganized thinking, and impairments in social functioning. Individuals experiencing psychosis may have difficulty distinguishing between what is real and what is not, leading to a distorted perception of the world around them.

On the other hand, a psychotic breakdown is a more acute and severe manifestation of psychosis. It often represents a tipping point where an individual's ability to cope with their symptoms becomes overwhelmed, resulting in a significant disruption of their daily life. During a psychotic breakdown, individuals may experience a complete loss of touch with reality, leading to extreme emotional distress, confusion, and even a potential risk to themselves or others. It is crucial to intervene promptly during a psychotic breakdown to ensure the individual's safety and provide appropriate treatment.

While the exact causes of psychosis and psychotic breakdowns are still not fully understood, research suggests a combination of genetic, environmental, and neurochemical factors may contribute to their development. Certain mental illnesses, such as schizophrenia and bipolar disorder, are commonly associated with psychosis and an increased risk of psychotic breakdowns. Substance abuse, sleep deprivation, and significant stress can also trigger or exacerbate these conditions.

Recovering from a psychotic breakdown requires a comprehensive approach that includes medical intervention, therapy, and support from loved ones. Medications, such as antipsychotics, can help manage the symptoms of psychosis, while therapy, such as cognitive-behavioral therapy, can assist individuals in understanding and challenging their distorted beliefs. Building a strong support network, including family, friends, and mental health professionals, is crucial for long-term recovery.

In conclusion, understanding the difference between psychosis and a psychotic breakdown is essential for individuals, their families, and caregivers. Psychosis refers to a broader symptom of mental disorders characterized by a loss of touch with reality, while a psychotic breakdown represents a severe episode of psychosis that disrupts daily functioning. By recognizing the signs, seeking prompt intervention, and providing ongoing support, individuals can navigate the complexities of psychotic breakdowns and work towards recovery.

Can psychosis be cured?

One of the most pressing questions for individuals experiencing a psychotic breakdown, their loved ones, and caregivers is whether psychosis can be cured. While the journey towards recovery may vary for each person, it is important to understand that psychosis can be effectively managed and treated, allowing individuals to regain control of their lives.

Psychosis refers to a mental health condition characterized by a loss of touch with reality, often accompanied by hallucinations, delusions, disorganized thoughts, and difficulties with social interactions. It can be a frightening and bewildering experience for those affected, as well as their families and friends.

The good news is that with timely intervention and appropriate treatment, many individuals with psychosis can experience significant improvement and lead fulfilling lives. It is crucial to emphasize that recovery from psychosis is not an overnight process, but rather a journey that requires dedication, support, and patience.

Treatment options for psychosis typically involve a combination of medication, therapy, and psychosocial support. Antipsychotic medications are commonly prescribed to manage symptoms and restore a balanced brain chemistry. These medications can effectively reduce hallucinations, delusions, and thought disturbances. However, it is important to work closely with a healthcare professional to find the right medication, as different individuals may respond differently to various options.

Therapy plays a crucial role in helping individuals with psychosis understand their condition and develop coping strategies. Cognitive-behavioral therapy (CBT) has been found particularly effective in addressing the cognitive distortions and negative thought patterns associated with psychosis. Family therapy can also be beneficial, as it provides education and support to both the individual and their loved ones.

In addition to medical and therapeutic interventions, psychosocial support is essential for long-term recovery. This can include vocational rehabilitation, housing support, and assistance with social integration. Building a strong support network, including family, friends, and support groups, is also vital in maintaining stability and preventing relapses.

While a complete cure for psychosis may not yet be available, the goal of treatment is to manage symptoms, improve quality of life, and empower individuals to live meaningful lives. With early intervention, comprehensive treatment plans, and ongoing support, individuals experiencing psychosis can find hope and navigate their way towards recovery.

It is important to remember that each person's journey is unique, and progress may vary. However, by understanding the available treatment options and the potential for improvement, individuals with psychosis, their families, and caregivers can approach the challenges of this condition with optimism and resilience.

How can I support someone going through a psychotic breakdown?

Witnessing a loved one or a friend experiencing a psychotic breakdown can be a challenging and distressing situation. It is crucial to remember that with the right support and understanding, individuals can recover and regain stability. In this subchapter, we will explore practical ways to provide assistance during this difficult time.

First and foremost, it is essential to educate yourself about psychotic breakdowns, their causes, symptoms, and recovery options. By understanding the condition, you can better empathize with the person experiencing it and respond appropriately. Additionally, seeking professional advice and guidance is highly recommended. Mental health professionals can provide valuable insights and guidance tailored to the specific needs of the individual.

Supporting someone through a psychotic breakdown requires patience, empathy, and non-judgmental listening. Encourage open communication and create a safe and non-threatening environment for them to share their thoughts and feelings. Active listening involves paying attention, asking clarifying questions, and expressing empathy. This approach can help build trust and foster a sense of support.

During a psychotic breakdown, individuals may struggle with daily tasks and self-care. Offering practical assistance with everyday activities such as cooking, cleaning, and personal hygiene can be tremendously helpful. This support allows them to focus on their recovery without feeling overwhelmed by basic responsibilities.

Encourage the person to engage in activities that promote relaxation and self-care, such as exercise, meditation, and hobbies they enjoy. These activities can serve as healthy distractions and outlets for stress reduction. Additionally, maintaining a regular sleep schedule and a balanced diet can contribute to their overall well-being.

It is important to understand that recovery is a process that takes time. Encourage them to stay consistent with their treatment plan and medication regimen. Offer to accompany them to therapy sessions or doctor appointments, if they feel comfortable. Be patient and understanding, as setbacks may occur, but remind them of their progress and achievements.

Lastly, take care of yourself. Supporting someone through a psychotic breakdown can be emotionally demanding. Ensure you have a support system in place and seek your own mental health support if needed. Remember that you cannot pour from an empty cup, and taking care of yourself allows you to provide better support to others.

In conclusion, supporting someone through a psychotic breakdown requires a combination of education, empathy, and practical assistance. By understanding the condition, offering a listening ear, and providing practical support, you can significantly aid in their recovery journey. Remember to be patient, encourage self-care, and seek support for yourself. Together, we can navigate the challenges of psychotic breakdowns and support those in need.

Chapter 10: Resources and Support

National and International Organizations

In the realm of mental health, national and international organizations play a crucial role in providing support, advocacy, and resources to individuals experiencing psychotic breakdowns and their loved ones. These organizations are dedicated to improving mental health services, raising awareness, and facilitating research to advance our understanding of psychotic breakdowns, their causes, symptoms, and recovery options. Here, we will explore some prominent national and international organizations that provide valuable assistance to the general public, patients, parents, and carers affected by psychotic breakdowns.

National organizations focused on mental health, such as the National Alliance on Mental Illness (NAMI) in the United States, offer a wide range of resources, support groups, and educational programs for individuals affected by psychotic breakdowns. NAMI's Family-to-Family Education Program, for instance, provides comprehensive information on various mental health conditions, including psychosis, and equips family members with the necessary tools to support their loved ones on the path to recovery.

Internationally, organizations like the World Health Organization (WHO) are committed to promoting mental health and well-being worldwide. The WHO provides valuable information on mental health conditions, including psychosis, and offers guidance on effective treatment options. Additionally, they work towards reducing the stigma associated with mental illnesses, encouraging individuals to seek help without fear of judgment or discrimination.

Another prominent organization is the Schizophrenia and Related Disorders Alliance of America (SARDAA), which focuses specifically on schizophrenia and related disorders. SARDAA provides support, education, and advocacy for individuals affected by psychotic breakdowns, as well as their families and caregivers. They offer various programs, including support groups and educational webinars, to empower individuals to lead fulfilling lives despite their challenges.

Furthermore, the International Society for Psychological and Social Approaches to Psychosis (ISPS) brings together professionals, researchers, and individuals with lived experiences to promote psychological and social approaches to psychosis treatment. ISPS organizes international conferences, publishes research papers, and advocates for holistic and person-centered care for those experiencing psychotic breakdowns.

Whether you are a patient, a parent, or a caregiver, these national and international organizations provide a wealth of knowledge and support to help you navigate the complexities of psychotic breakdowns. By accessing their resources, attending support groups, and engaging with their programs, you can find comfort, guidance, and hope on your journey towards recovery and well-being.

Online Support Communities

In today's digital age, the internet has revolutionized the way we connect and communicate with others. This has led to the emergence of online support communities, which have become invaluable resources for individuals experiencing a psychotic breakdown, as well as their loved ones. These communities provide a safe and supportive space for individuals to share their experiences, seek advice, and find solace in the company of others who can relate to their struggles.

For those going through a psychotic breakdown, it is not uncommon to feel isolated and misunderstood. However, by engaging with online support communities, individuals can find a sense of belonging and validation. These communities are often comprised of individuals who have firsthand experience with psychotic breakdowns, making them uniquely qualified to provide insights and empathy. Whether you are seeking information about symptoms, causes, or treatment options, these communities can offer a wealth of knowledge and support.

One of the greatest advantages of online support communities is the ability to remain anonymous. This allows individuals to freely express their thoughts and emotions without fear of judgment or stigma. Patients, parents, and carers can openly discuss their concerns, ask questions, and receive advice from others who have faced similar challenges. The sense of understanding and compassion within these communities can be incredibly empowering, providing individuals with a renewed sense of hope and motivation.

Moreover, online support communities can help individuals navigate the recovery process. Members often share their stories of resilience and healing, offering inspiration and guidance to those who may be feeling overwhelmed or discouraged. By connecting with others who have successfully overcome a psychotic breakdown, individuals can gain valuable insights into coping strategies, treatment options, and self-care practices. This shared wisdom can be instrumental in promoting a sense of empowerment and agency in the recovery journey.

It is important to note that while online support communities can be a valuable resource, they should not replace professional medical advice or treatment. These communities should be viewed as complementary to traditional therapy and medication, providing additional support and a sense of community. It is always advisable to consult with a qualified healthcare professional for personalized guidance and treatment.

In conclusion, online support communities have become vital lifelines for individuals experiencing a psychotic breakdown, as well as their loved ones. These communities offer a safe and supportive space to share experiences, seek advice, and find solace in the company of others who can relate. By engaging with these communities, individuals can find a sense of belonging, validation, and inspiration on their journey towards recovery.

Recommended Books and Websites

As you navigate the challenging journey of understanding and coping with psychotic breakdown, it is essential to arm yourself with knowledge and resources that can support you along the way. This subchapter presents a curated list of recommended books and websites that cater to a diverse audience, including the general public, patients, parents, and carers. These resources encompass various aspects of psychotic breakdown, including its causes, symptoms, and recovery options. Whether you are seeking personal insight, guidance, or practical advice, these sources can serve as valuable companions throughout your quest for understanding and healing.

Books:

1. "I Am Not Sick, I Don't Need Help!" by Xavier Amador, Ph.D.
Dr. Amador's groundbreaking book offers invaluable advice for families and caregivers on how to effectively communicate with individuals experiencing psychosis and help them access treatment.

2. "The Center Cannot Hold: My Journey Through Madness" by Elyn R. Saks
This memoir provides a firsthand account of Elyn Saks' struggle with schizophrenia and her eventual triumph over the disorder. It offers a unique perspective from someone who has experienced psychosis while also being an expert in mental health law.

3. "Surviving Schizophrenia: A Family Manual" by E. Fuller Torrey, M.D.
Dr. Torrey's comprehensive guide is an indispensable resource for patients, families, and caregivers. It covers all aspects of schizophrenia, including symptoms, treatment options, and strategies for supporting recovery.

Websites:

1. National Alliance on Mental Illness (NAMI) - www.nami.org
NAMI is a leading grassroots organization that provides support, education, and advocacy for individuals and families affected by mental health conditions. Their website offers a wealth of information, resources, and helplines for various mental health disorders, including psychosis.

2. Schizophrenia and Related Disorders Alliance of America (SARDAA) - www.sardaa.org

SARDAA is dedicated to improving the lives of individuals affected by schizophrenia and related disorders. Their website features educational materials, personal stories, and support resources for patients, families, and professionals.

3. Mind - www.mind.org.uk
Mind is a UK-based mental health charity that aims to empower individuals and promote mental well-being. Their website provides reliable information on various mental health conditions, including psychosis, along with practical tips for coping and accessing support.

Remember, these recommended books and websites are not meant to replace professional guidance or treatment, but rather to supplement your understanding and provide additional support. Always consult with qualified medical professionals for personalized advice and treatment options.

Introduction:
In this subchapter, we would like to address the fact that the book outline provided is intended as a general guide. We understand that each individual's experience with psychotic breakdown may be unique, and specific requirements and research findings may warrant modifications or expansions to the information provided. Our goal is to provide a comprehensive overview of psychotic breakdown, its causes, symptoms, and available treatment options, while also acknowledging the need for flexibility and customization in addressing individual needs.

Understanding Psychotic Breakdown:
In this section, we will delve into the concept of psychotic breakdown, offering a clear definition and exploring its various manifestations. We will discuss the potential causes, which can include genetic predisposition, environmental factors, and substance abuse. It is important to note that while these causes are commonly observed, individual experiences may vary, and additional research

findings may contribute to a more nuanced understanding of the condition.

Symptoms and Warning Signs:
This section will focus on identifying the symptoms and warning signs of a psychotic breakdown. We will explore common symptoms such as hallucinations, delusions, disorganized thinking, and impaired social functioning. Additionally, we will emphasize the importance of recognizing early warning signs to facilitate early intervention and improved outcomes.

Treatment Options:
In this section, we will discuss the various treatment options available for individuals experiencing a psychotic breakdown. We will explore both pharmacological interventions, such as antipsychotic medications, as well as non-pharmacological approaches, including therapy, social support, and lifestyle modifications. It is crucial to highlight that treatment plans should be tailored to individual needs and preferences, and may require adjustments based on research findings and advancements in the field.

Conclusion:
While the book outline provided offers a general guide to understanding and navigating psychotic breakdown, it is essential to acknowledge that each person's experience may require modifications or expansions based on specific requirements and research findings. By remaining open to new information and individual needs, we can ensure that this book serves as a valuable resource for the general public, patients, parents, and carers seeking knowledge and guidance on psychotic breakdown, its causes, symptoms, and recovery.

Unraveling the Mysteries of a Psychotic Breakdown: Causes, Symptoms, and Recovery

The human mind, while a remarkable marvel, can sometimes succumb to extraordinary challenges that push it to the brink. A psychotic breakdown, a profoundly disruptive episode of mental distress, can shatter the delicate balance of reality and plunge individuals into a tumultuous realm of confusion and distress. In this article, we will delve into the intricate layers of a psychotic breakdown, shedding light on its causes, symptoms, and the path to recovery.

Understanding the Landscape

A psychotic breakdown, often referred to as a psychotic episode, is a period of intense mental turmoil where an individual's grasp on reality becomes distorted. This break from reality can manifest in a variety of ways, including hallucinations, delusions, disorganized thoughts, and impaired functioning. The underlying causes of a psychotic breakdown are complex and multifaceted, involving a combination of genetic, environmental, and neurological factors.

Causes of a Psychotic Breakdown

1. **Genetic Predisposition:** A family history of mental disorders can increase the risk of experiencing a psychotic breakdown, suggesting a genetic link to susceptibility.

2. **Neurochemical Imbalances:** Disruptions in brain chemistry, particularly involving neurotransmitters like dopamine, have been associated with the onset of psychotic symptoms.

3. **Stress and Trauma:** Severe emotional stress, trauma, or significant life changes can trigger or exacerbate a psychotic episode in vulnerable individuals.

4. **Substance Abuse:** The misuse of drugs or alcohol can amplify the risk of a psychotic breakdown, often exacerbating existing mental health conditions.

5. **Neurological Factors:** Certain neurological conditions, such as epilepsy or brain injuries, can contribute to the development of psychotic symptoms.

Recognizing the Symptoms

Symptoms of a psychotic breakdown can vary widely and may include:

- **Hallucinations:** Sensing things that are not present, such as hearing voices or seeing things that others do not.
- **Delusions:** Holding false, irrational beliefs that are resistant to reasoning or evidence.
- **Disorganized Thinking:** Incoherent speech, difficulty concentrating, and disjointed thought patterns.
- **Impaired Social Functioning:** Withdrawal from relationships and difficulty communicating with others.
- **Erratic Behavior:** Unpredictable actions that may be influenced by delusions or hallucinations.

The Road to Recovery

Recovering from a psychotic breakdown often requires a comprehensive and multidimensional approach:

1. **Medical Intervention:** A combination of antipsychotic medications and mood stabilizers can help alleviate symptoms and stabilize mood.

2. **Therapeutic Support:** Psychotherapy, such as cognitive-behavioral therapy (CBT) or dialectical behavior therapy (DBT), can help individuals develop coping strategies and manage symptoms.

3. **Supportive Environment:** A strong support network of family, friends, and mental health professionals is essential for providing understanding and encouragement.

4. **Lifestyle Adjustments:** Adopting a healthy lifestyle, including proper sleep, regular exercise, and a balanced diet, can contribute to overall mental well-being.

5. **Education and Coping Skills:** Learning about the condition, its triggers, and practicing mindfulness techniques can empower individuals to navigate and manage symptoms.

Breaking the Stigma

As we unravel the complexities of a psychotic breakdown, it's crucial to remember that mental health is an integral part of overall well-being. By fostering open conversations and promoting awareness, we can shatter the stigma surrounding mental illness and provide a compassionate space for those who have experienced a psychotic breakdown to seek help and embark on a journey towards healing and recovery.

Beyond Reality: Exploring Visual and Auditory Hallucinations

The human mind is a remarkable landscape, capable of producing vivid experiences that shape our perception of reality. However, there are moments when this finely tuned instrument falters, leading to extraordinary phenomena like visual and auditory hallucinations. In this article, we embark on a journey to understand these intriguing distortions of perception, exploring their nature, causes, and the insights they offer into the complex workings of the human brain.

Defining Visual and Auditory Hallucinations

Visual hallucinations involve seeing things that aren't present in the external environment, while auditory hallucinations manifest as hearing sounds or voices that lack any external source. These sensory distortions can be bewildering, blurring the line between what's real and what's imagined.

The Mind's Theater: Visual Hallucinations

1. **Nature of Visual Hallucinations:** Visual hallucinations can take various forms, from fleeting shadows and distorted shapes to detailed scenes and vibrant colors.

2. **Causes and Triggers:** Visual hallucinations can be triggered by conditions like schizophrenia, Parkinson's disease, migraines, and even sleep disorders.

3. **Influence of the Brain:** Research suggests that visual hallucinations may result from the brain's attempt to interpret random neural activity in the visual cortex, crafting it into coherent images.

Whispers in the Mind: Auditory Hallucinations

1. **Auditory Hallucination Spectrum:** Auditory hallucinations range from hearing indistinct noises to experiencing vivid, detailed voices speaking or even conversing.

2. **Rooted in Mental Health:** Auditory hallucinations are often associated with conditions like schizophrenia, but they can also be experienced during extreme stress, sleep deprivation, and certain medical conditions.

3. **The Brain's Orchestra:** Auditory hallucinations may arise from abnormal activity in the brain's auditory cortex, with the brain interpreting its own signals as external sounds.

Connecting the Dots: Possible Overlaps

Interestingly, there can be cases where visual and auditory hallucinations intertwine, creating an even more intricate cognitive landscape. The brain's attempts to make sense of mixed signals can result in rich, multidimensional experiences that challenge our understanding of reality.

The Window into Neurodiversity

Visual and auditory hallucinations can offer valuable insights into the complexities of neurodiversity:

1. **Understanding Brain Variability:** The wide spectrum of hallucination experiences underscores the unique ways our brains process information.

2. **Highlighting Mental Health:** Hallucinations often accompany conditions like schizophrenia and bipolar disorder, shedding light on the challenges faced by individuals with these conditions.

3. **Empathy and Compassion:** Learning about hallucinations fosters empathy and understanding, breaking down stigmas surrounding mental health and creating a more compassionate society.

Conclusion

Visual and auditory hallucinations remind us that the human mind is a universe of its own, capable of both brilliant clarity and intriguing distortion. By delving into the complexities of these phenomena, we gain insight into the intricate mechanisms that shape our perceptions and interactions with the world around us. As we continue to explore the realms of neuroscience and psychology, let us approach the topic with open minds and hearts, extending compassion to those whose experiences may differ from our own.